HANDICAPPING
CONTEST
HANDBOOK

HANDICAPPING CONTEST HANDBOOK

A HORSEPLAYER'S GUIDE TO HANDICAPPING TOURNAMENTS

by

Noel Michaels

DRF Press

NEW YORK

Published by
Daily Racing Form Press
100 Broadway, 7th Floor
New York, NY 10005

ISBN: 0-9700147-4-0
Library of Congress Control Number: 2002114411

Cover and jacket designed by Chris Donofry

Text design by Neuwirth and Associates

Printed in the United States of America

Contents

CONTENTS

CONTENTS

Acknowledgments

*T*HANKS TO THE following for their help with this book:

From *Daily Racing Form* and DRF Press, I'd like to thank Charlie Hayward, Steven Crist, Robin Foster, Mandy Minger, Dean Keppler, Chris Donofry, Geoff Faustman, Steve Marcinak, Dave Tuley, Glenye Cain, Steve Andersen, Bill Tallon, and publicists Tim O'Leary and Scott Cooper. Thanks to Keith Chamblin, Jamie Haydon, Eric Wing, and everyone else at the NTRA. Thanks to all of the people I asked to contribute in this book including Robert Bertolucci, David Crupi, John Curran, Ken Daniels, J. Randy Gallo, Ross Gallo, Joe Girardi (the handicapper, not the catcher), Dave Gutfreund, Joe Hinson, Mike Labriola, Ralph Siroco, Jeff Sotman, and Steve Terelak. I'd like to thank my friends, David Abrams, John G. Dooley, and Mitchell Garfinkel. I also wish to acknowledge all of the people who helped me gather information for this book including Chris Andrews (Cal-Neva Casino), John Avello (Bally's-Las Vegas), Chris Bahr (Del Mar), Kim Bahrami (Cal Expo), Don Barberino (Autotote), Liza Markle Bell (Hoosier), Cyril Berger (Las Vegas Hilton), Amelia Blanco (Turf Paradise), Mary Lou Day Cody (Prairie Meadows), Jim Corbett and the staff of *American Turf Monthly*, Robert Cunningham (Ellis Park), Adam Dudley (NYRA), Steve Fierro (Reno Hilton), Debbie Flaig (Orleans Race Book), Vince Francia (Turf Paradise), Ray Henry (Bettor Racing OTB), Jolynn Johnston

ACKNOWLEDGMENTS

(River Downs), Donna Kane, Carrie La Rue (Prairie Meadows), Keith Leacock (Maryland Jockey Club), Richard Linihan (Fair Meadows), M. Scott McMannis (Sportsman's Park), Jeff Maday (Canterbury Park), Chris Meeks (Sam Houston), Paul Messell, Dick Moore (Horsemen's Park), Bill Nader (NYRA), Jeff Scarfo (NYRA), Larry Sinclair (Twin Spires Club), Susie Sourwine (Emerald Downs), Joe Sweet (Suffolk Downs), Felix Taverna, Jeff True (Los Alamitos), the University of Arizona Race Track Industry Program, Lenny Vangilder (Fair Grounds), "Mr." Ed Weigand, the Westin Resort in St. John, U.S.V.I. (where Chapter 4 was written), and Darrell Wood (Colonial Downs).

Many thanks to Phil (P. G.), Mary Kay, and Kathy Johnson, and Don, Emma, and Carolyn Brockway, and Volponi, for all being so good to me.

A very special thanks to my mom and dad, Norman and Velda, and my wife, Karen M. Johnson, for all their love, support, patience, and devotion.

HANDICAPPING CONTEST HANDBOOK

1

INTRODUCTION

FOR THE INCREASING number of handicapping-contest enthusiasts popping up at racetracks from coast to coast, nothing seems to beat the fun and excitement of tournament play.

Handicapping contests give horseplayers a chance to test their skills and see how they measure up against other players at their home track, or all over the country. If you think you're the best horse handicapper there is, or at least the best contest player, there is no better way to prove it than by winning a tournament.

Handicapping contests and tournaments are not for everyone. They are for that special breed of horseplayer that craves the excitement, competition, and adrenaline rush associated with going head to head with some of the best handicappers in the game. Tournaments have become a big part of the world of handicapping, and they're only getting bigger as more and more players become attracted to the thrill of competing in this growing segment of Thoroughbred racing.

Handicapping tournaments are their own separate sport within a sport, with their own rules, their own players, and their own keys to success.

Every day at the racetrack is a competition of sorts between you and your fellow bettors. That, after all, is the basis of all parimutuel wagering. Contests, however, take their participants above parimutuel wagering's level of competition into a world where handicapping, and not betting, is the name of the game. Handicapping contests provide a competitive environment far beyond what you would experience in a normal day at the track.

These days, there is a handicapping contest or tournament being held somewhere just about every weekend, and keeping up with the who, what, where, and when of these contests can be nearly as difficult as actually understanding how to win. This handbook is meant to serve not only as a source of information on how to find the handicapping contests that are right for you, but also as a guide to developing winning strategies.

Why have handicapping tournaments become so popular, not only with handicappers everywhere, but also with the racetracks, OTB's, casinos, and web sites that host them? One of the big reasons is the added value that contests offer horseplayers who are not normally accustomed to perks and special treatment by racetracks. Often contests even become a way to bet on racing without a takeout.

Value is a big reason why tournaments are so popular now, but that certainly isn't the only reason. After all, tournaments have always offered good value. The other main reason tournaments have exploded in popularity in recent years has been the creation of the Daily Racing Form/NTRA National Handicapping Championship. The national championship event for horseplayers, which has been held every January since 2000 in Las Vegas, has already become an institution within the sport of horse racing.

The National Handicapping Championship not only offers a purse of more than $200,000, but also gives its winner national recognition as the year's top horseplayer, and the title of DRF/NTRA Handicapper of the Year.

One of the great things about the National Handicapping Championship is that it is not restricted to so-called professionals and experts. It's open to every racing fan from the turf club to the grandstand, no matter if he bets $2 a race or $2,000. It is handicapping's equivalent of the U.S. Open. Anyone can qualify.

This handbook will attempt to bring you inside the world of horse handicapping contests, beginning with a brief history of tournaments, and ending with an index of every major contest now being held in every part of the country.

Not all handicapping contests are created equal. Wagering formats, purse structures, rules, and procedures differ from one contest to another.

This guide will try to explain the different types of contests and the pluses and minuses associated with each of them.

Finally, and most importantly, this guide contains advice meant to give you an edge on your competition. It includes strategy on how to become a winning tournament player as well as tips from some of the top handicappers in the game.

This guide is meant to be a constant companion for you as you try to navigate the long, winding road to the DRF/NTRA National Handicapping Championship. The second half of this book contains a rundown of each National Handicapping Championship qualifying tournament currently on the DRF/NTRA NHC annual schedule. In addition to basic information, this handy index will provide a brief synopsis of each qualifying event, including tips on how to win and advance to the greatest show in all of Thoroughbred handicapping, the Daily Racing Form/NTRA National Handicapping Championship.

The index of contests is something you can refer to over and over again throughout the year as you prepare your personal plan of attack.

BECOMING A TOURNAMENT PLAYER

Contests and tournaments are popular for some of the same reasons that pick sixes and superfectas are popular. Horse bettors want a chance to bet a little to win a lot. You may have to go a long time between wins, but when you eventually hit it big, the jackpot can be in the tens of thousands of dollars.

TOP REASONS FOR THE POPULARITY OF HANDICAPPING CONTESTS:

- DRF/NTRA National Handicapping Championship
- Recognition for handicappers
- Value, often with no takeout
- Benefit both hosts and handicappers
- Camaraderie
- Competition
- Action-packed events

THE NATIONAL HANDICAPPING CHAMPIONSHIP

Each year, an estimated 45,000 entrants participate in the qualifying process for the National Handicapping Championship. However, there are only about 200 open slots in the national finals. This means that only the few best—and/or luckiest—Thoroughbred handicappers will make it to handicapping's annual showcase event.

Since the onset of the DRF/NTRA National Handicapping Championship, horseplayers and handicappers have had something akin to their own national tour, which stretches all over the country throughout the year. In 2002, 48 different tracks, OTB's, casinos, web sites, and organizations held local stand-alone contests that also served as regional qualifying events for the national championship.

Not all tournaments on the annual calendar are affiliated with the DRF/NTRA NHC, but many players now give priority to playing in the contests that are qualifying events for the national contest. The wide-spread appeal of the one true year-end national-championship contest is among the primary reasons that handicapping contests have mush-roomed in popularity in recent years.

RECOGNITION FOR HANDICAPPERS

Since 2000, the National Handicapping Championship has brought the winners of dozens of regional contests together in Las Vegas for a climac-tic event that crowns horse racing's national champion handicapper, a.k.a. the DRF/NTRA Handicapper of the Year. Just like horse racing's other year-end champions—both human and equine—the champion handicap-per is honored at the Eclipse Awards alongside other top figures in the sport of horse racing, such as owners, breeders, trainers, and jockeys.

The winner of the national contest not only earns the first prize of $100,000, but also the title of Daily Racing Form/NTRA Handicapper of the Year. This is priceless recognition as a representative for all horse-players, and an acknowledgment that bettors have as big a part in horse racing as the other participants.

Value
One of the biggest things that attracts horseplayers to handicapping contests is the value they offer as opposed to an average day at the track. In a crowded gaming landscape filled with high takeouts and costly

overhead, contests are a good value-added alternative to other forms of handicapping and betting. Contests offer you the chance to place a bet on your own abilities—often at a zero-percent takeout—while also giving you the opportunity to make a big score.

From a bettor's perspective, the offering of a zero-takeout betting option is huge considering that the massive gaming resorts in Las Vegas and elsewhere were built on the small-percentage house advantages programmed into every slot machine and table game on the casino floor. Even sports bettors must go up against the house's 4.54 percent cut, known as the "vig," taken out of every winning bet to slide the odds back in the house's favor.

Those who bet parimutuel sports such as horse racing or dog racing, whether they are playing at the track or at a race book, know all too well that they are playing against one of the biggest house advantages anywhere. The takeout on horse racing ranges from 15 to 30 percent of every dollar wagered, depending on the type of bet and the takeout laws of individual racing jurisdictions.

Above and beyond the takeout, racing fans who attend the track on a regular basis also must overcome additional overhead costs in order to break even. Track-goers can generally expect to start their day by paying for parking or for transportation to the track and then paying admission to get in.

Bettors also need some handicapping information in order to play the races, so add on the cost of a *Daily Racing Form* and whatever other information you like to purchase.

Since the average Thoroughbred race card lasts somewhere around four hours, you'll probably want to eat or drink something while you're playing the races. That's at least another few bucks you're in the hole before facing that 15-to-30 percent takeout they hit you with in order to finance purses, pay taxes, and turn a profit.

Based on typical takeouts ranging from 15 to 30 percent, you'll be giving the track anywhere from $150 to $300 dollars a day if you're the type of bettor who wagers $1,000. Aside from the takeout, nonbetting overhead expenses for one day at the track may end up averaging $25 or more, thanks to parking, admission, and food costs.

Of course, not everyone pays for parking, admission, and food anymore. The majority of tracks now offer players' clubs and high-rollers' rooms that cater to the biggest and most frequent players. The concept of rewarding high rollers began at casinos and has slowly made its way to racetracks over the years. Casinos regularly award their biggest players free meals, free rooms, free shows, free this and free that. And now, with the use of player-tracking technology, tracks have begun to catch on to this idea and to offer their biggest bettors perks including admission to their own private, deluxe room, parking, meals, and points that can be redeemed for merchandise and other things of value to handicappers.

The problem is that the average player doesn't bet enough money to qualify for a track's high-rollers' club and therefore does not have access to these perks. If you do bet enough to qualify for high-roller status, the few bucks you might lose here and there on parking and admission probably won't mean as much to you as the thousands of dollars lost to takeouts.

That's where handicapping contests come in.

Handicapping contests as we know them today originated in Las Vegas race books, so it's no surprise that they usually include several value-added features to attract horseplayers.

First and foremost, tournaments are a better betting proposition than parimutuel wagering because there is often no takeout. Many of the top contests pay back 100 percent of all entry fees in the form of prize money. This is the reason horseplayers are so willing to plunk down entry fees that can range anywhere from $2 to $3,000 in order to participate.

Additionally, all of the perks mentioned above are usually thrown in at no charge at tournaments, making them an even greater deal for horse-players. Almost every contest out there now offers its entrants free meals, free beverages (occasionally including alcohol), free *Daily Racing Form*s, and sometimes a free gift such as a hat or a shirt. Contests at racetracks also usually offer free parking, admission, and a program for the day.

A zero takeout alone is a great advantage to playing in tournaments, but many events don't stop there. Some contests go the extra mile by kicking in funds of their own for additional prize money. This often takes the form of daily prize money, or goes into a separate pool to be used for an early-bird tournament held the day before or the day after the main event.

In short, tournaments change horse-playing from a negative proposition into a positive one. By selectively playing in contests with no take-out, enthusiasts can give themselves a real chance to achieve a long-term positive return on their tournament investment, while all along being treated like a high roller in the process. Not a bad deal.

With so much to offer, it's no wonder that handicapping tournaments have attracted the attention of so many horseplayers who now can be treated to a game with favorable odds and take a break from the usual day-to-day fleecing they have come to expect from racetracks.

BENEFIT BOTH HOSTS AND HANDICAPPERS

No matter how much the players may want handicapping contests to be offered to them by tracks and race books, the contests probably wouldn't exist unless they were also a good deal for the hosts as well as the players.

From the tracks' point of view, tournaments are offered primarily to reward their regular customers who are becoming increasingly interested in competing in tournaments. Contests are also used as a marketing tool to introduce and attract new players to their facilities. Tracks prefer larger on-track handle and attendance because they make more money from bets made on-track than they do from those made off-track. On-track fans also spend money eating, drinking, parking, etc., and the track would rather get that money than see it go to someone else.

Thanks to the draw of handicapping contests, tracks can attract fans who might normally go to OTB's or sit at home and wager via their phone accounts or on their computers. The reverse is true for OTB's and casinos. Off-track outlets can use contests as a tool to draw people away from the tracks and into their race books.

Tracks or OTB's have countless choices as to how to spend their marketing budgets. They can use that money to put up a billboard, or they can spend it on a handicapping contest. There's no way to tell how much something like a billboard will increase business, but there's no doubt about how much name recognition, goodwill, and handle can be increased thanks to a well-run contest.

The types of bettors who play in tournaments are usually the core parimutuel bettors whom tracks and OTB's love to have around. These aren't two-dollar bettors. These are the big per-capita bettors. They are the 10 percent of all players who account for 90 percent of handle. Contests often bring their hosts an influx of big bettors. When the big bettors are in the house, a host has an excellent chance to put its best foot forward to try to turn its tournament guests into regular customers, or at least occasional visitors.

Even if a contest fails to boost a facility's long-term business, it should at least provide a noticeable short-term shot in the arm for on-track handle. This is true whether a tournament is run through the parimutuel tote system or not. Handle is sure to be increased at any given venue by just having big-betting tournament players around for a day or two.

Competition

When you get right down to it, every parimutuel bet made every day at every racetrack is a competition of sorts. Bets change the odds and odds determine the payoffs, and when you collect, you're being paid with money that comes from losing bettors rather than from the house. Parimutuel betting is competitive, but it's a nameless, faceless competition on an abstract playing field. Conversely, handicapping tournaments put your adversaries right in front of you and create a competitive arena for horseplayers to test their skills against one another in head-to-head combat.

Camaraderie

Camaraderie cannot be overlooked as a major factor in the allure of handicapping contests. Players who meet at contests often find that they have a lot more in common than just a shared enjoyment of tournament play. The competitors get to know each other over time and often become good friends with their tournament rivals. Avid tournament players who come from different parts of the country may see one another several times a year at the many large-scale events across the nation. Many of the most frequent tournament players know each other, and use these contests as a convenient time, place, and reason to renew their acquaintance, year in and year out.

Action

There is nothing quite like the atmosphere at a well-run, competitive handicapping tournament. What could possibly be better action than cramming 100 or more boisterous handicappers into a room and putting large amounts of prize money up for grabs to the winners? We're not talking about the kind of contests that involve picking winners and dropping an entry blank into a drum. We're talking about a competitive atmosphere akin to sporting events complete with scoreboards and continuous action coming from every corner of the venue. When tournaments bring together handicappers and offer them simulcast action from several locations, the atmosphere can become electric.

2

TOURNAMENT TIMELINE

HORSE HANDICAPPING TOURNAMENTS are at the pinnacle of their popularity, but also have a long and interesting history dating back to the mid-1970's. Here's a look at just a few of the high points, and low points, in the history of handicapping contests, beginning at a small track in eastern Pennsylvania and ending in Las Vegas with the Daily Racing Form/NTRA National Handicapping Championship.

OCTOBER 1976—The first major handicapping contest, the *World Series of Handicapping*, was created at Penn National Racecourse. The track's publicity director, Kelso Sturgeon, came up with the idea of an annual handicapping "world series" to coincide with baseball's World Series in late October. The first World Series of Handicapping drew 189 players who competed for a purse of $7,000 in a winner-take-all event. Over the years, the contest grew into a major $205,500 event consisting of as many as five preliminary rounds with 150 entrants in each. The top 24 finishers in each preliminary advanced to the finals, where they met two dozen invited professionals and the winners of other assorted handicapping contests at far-flung racetracks. Winners earned a grand prize of $100,000, and payoffs were made down to fifth place. Despite the presence of dozens of invited turf writers and professional players over the years, no nonqualifying invited player won the event until 1995.

JULY 1982—Mike and Barry Lavine of Worldwide Tournament Consultants Inc. hosted their first handicapping contest at the race book at the MGM Grand-Reno. The tournament, later dubbed the *World Cup of Thoroughbred Handicapping*, lasted 16 years before its demise in 1998. That first contest in July 1982 was won by art-supply dealer **Howard DeMar**, who took home a grand prize of $82,000. Between 1982 and 1998, a total of 36 World Cups were held at several different hotel/casinos in both Las Vegas and Reno, including Caesar's Palace, the old MGM Grand, Bally's, the Sands, and the Palace Station. The World Series of Handicapping at Penn National preceded the World Cup by almost six years, but the Lavines are widely recognized as the ones who came up with the idea for handicapping contests as we've grown to know them today.

OCTOBER 1982—Handicapping author and *Washington Post* columnist Andrew Beyer was poised to become the first invited professional to win the *World Series of Handicapping* at Penn National with a seemingly insurmountable lead going into the final race of the three-day contest. Beyer's victory was not to be, however, as eventual winner **Paul Enriquez** wagered his entire bankroll in desperation on a winning 13-1 longshot in the final race of the contest to overtake Beyer and win the championship. This occurrence led to a rule change the following year at Penn National that limited wagers to 10 percent of a player's total bankroll in the last three races of the contest.

JUNE 1983—The *World Championship of Race Horse Handicapping* began its 18-year run at Club Cal-Neva Casino in Reno, Nevada. The real-money four-day contest, which was held in the Cal-Neva's Top Deck Race Book, remained one of the most popular handicapping contests in the country until its cancellation following the January 2000 edition. The format of the tournament changed very little over the years. Players started with $500 and made 10 bets a day, each equal to 10 percent of their total, on each day of the contest. Besides their own earnings, players vied for a $50,000 purse, which consisted primarily of house money. The biannual event topped out with 403 entrants in January 1995, and never drew fewer than 187 players, which was the attendance of the final contest. The World Championship was an annual attraction for some of the biggest tournament players in the country. Multiple winners of this tournament included **Jim Dempster** of Carson City, Nevada (twice), **Bill Wilbur** of Gault, California (twice), and **Valerie Hinson** (three-time winner) of Memphis, Tennessee.

OCTOBER 1992—One of the longest-lived handicapping tournaments in Nevada, the *Pick the Ponies Invitational*, began its run at the Superbook of the Las Vegas Hilton. The idea was to create a biannual contest centered around horse racing's two biggest days, the Kentucky Derby and the Breeders' Cup. The contest is currently still going strong with Pick the Ponies XX in May 2002 and Pick the Ponies XXI in October 2002 selling out 200 entries. The format of the Pick the Ponies Invitational has remained basically the same throughout its history, with the exception of a lowering of the entry fee from $600 to $500 in 1999. Players make 10 mythical $100 across-the-board wagers on 10 different races a day for three days. The winner earns 38 percent of the prize pool, or $38,000, based on a full field of 200. Payoffs are made down to 30th place.

OCTOBER 1995—*The World Series of Handicapping* was finally won by an invited media member. **Bill Handleman**, a columnist for the *Asbury Park Press* in New Jersey, took home first prize of $100,000 after compiling a contest-winning bankroll of $9,808 in the three-day tournament. The victory ended a 19-year drought by invited media members in the World Series. Roughly two dozen turf writers and handicappers were invited to the finals of the contest each year, and therefore did not need to advance to the finals by qualifying in one of Penn National's preliminary rounds. This practice was controversial, and in 1998, the new management of *Daily Racing Form* prohibited its employees from receiving preferential treatment in any tournament.

FEBRUARY 1997—Autotote hosted the first *Sports Haven Handicapping Challenge* at its Sports Haven teletheater in New Haven, Connecticut. The event was a smash hit right off the bat, selling out 300 spots and offering prize money of $60,000. The winner of that contest was North Haven, Connecticut, restaurant owner **Nicholas Scasino.** He earned first prize of $23,390.64 thanks, in part, to his selection of Frisk Me Now, who paid $213.80 in the Hutcheson Stakes at Gulfstream Park. A year later in 1998, Autotote added a second annual contest at the Hartford-area Bradley Teletheater. Together, the two Autotote contests have since unseated Penn National's World Series to become the biggest and most prestigious handicapping tournaments on the East Coast. The Sports Haven contest now offers prize money in excess of $100,000. Past winners have included **Bob Weidlich** (Sports Haven, 1998), **Rick Lang** (Sports Haven, 1999), **David Crupi** (Bradley, 1999), **Ron Butkiewicz** (Sports Haven, 2000), **John Gilberg** (Bradley, 2000), **Charles Carito** (Sports Haven, 2001), **Mike Labriola** (Bradley, 2001), **Stuart "Beef" Rubin** (Sports Haven, 2002), and **Tom Quigley** (Bradley, 2002). The Autotote contests are credited with popularizing the trend of bet-by-bet scorekeeping at contests, which has since become the norm at many events outside Nevada.

MARCH 1998—The inaugural *National Handicapping Challenge* was held at the race book at the Orleans in Las Vegas. The tournament was destined to become the biggest and most successful handicapping tournament ever held in terms of both prize money and participants. After 435 entrants played in the contest's first edition, the event quickly grew to 537 entries in October 1998, 600 entries in March 1999, 718 entries in October 1999, and 708 entries in March 2000. The reason for the contest's success was simple: Robert "Muggsy" Muniz, the director of racing for the Coast Resorts, including the Orleans, treated his customers as valued guests and put a premium on customer service at his tournaments. The Orleans not only returned 100 percent of all entry fees in the form of prize money, but also kicked in an additional $50,000 per contest for daily prizes and an early-bird contest. The first five winners of this event were (tournament points in parentheses): **Steve Duffy**, March 1998 ($11,080); **Ralph Siraco**, October 1998 ($9,148); **Ross and Randy Gallo**, March 1999 ($10,022); **Solomon Fiengold**, October 1999 ($10,194); and **Joe Hinson**, March 2000 ($9,222).

AUGUST 1998—*The Flamingo Hilton Reno Challenge* began its short-lived run as Reno's top handicapping tournament. After 87 entrants competed in the first contest in August 1998, Flamingo Reno race and sports-book manager Ed Weigand eventually turned the tournament into a major success story with as many as 370 players attend-

ing the event at its peak in February 2001. Weigand was a master pro-
moter of the contest, personally calling potential players and wooing
them with perks and freebies such as complimentary meals, rooms, and
limousine service to and from the hotel. The contest broke its own
attendance record each time it was held until it grew to be the second-
biggest tournament in Nevada behind only the National Handicapping
Challenge at the Orleans. Unfortunately, the tournament could not
survive the departure of Weigand from the Flamingo Reno in the
spring of 2001. Just as quickly as the contest appeared on the scene, it
flamed out of existence in July 2001 after just seven renewals.

JUNE 1999—*Daily Racing Form* and the National Thoroughbred Racing
Association announced the creation of the **National Handicapping
Championship**. The invitation-only event would feature qualifying
contests held at racetracks, casinos, and OTB's all over North America,
with the top four finishers from each regional event advancing to a gala
national final in Las Vegas. The purse was announced at $200,000,
with $100,000 and the title of DRF/NTRA Handicapper of the Year
going to the winner. Plans were also made for the eventual winner to
be honored at the Eclipse Award ceremonies. This would be the first
time a horseplayer would be recognized alongside the best jockeys,
trainers, owners, and breeders in Thoroughbred racing.

JUNE 1999—The first qualifying contest for the DRF/NTRA National
Handicapping Championship was held at **Foxwoods** casino in
southeastern Connecticut. The contest drew 153 handicappers and
was won by **David Morrone** of Westerly, Rhode Island, who offi-
cially became the first-ever qualifier to the National Handicapping
Championship finals.

JANUARY 2000—The inaugural ***DRF/NTRA National Handicapping Championship*** took place on January 7-8 at the MGM
Grand race and sports book in Las Vegas, Nevada. The $200,000
national championship was the culmination of months of qualifying
contests held at 40 participating racetracks, OTB's, and casinos in
North America. In all, 160 handicappers—140 men and 20
women—hailing from 27 states and Canada qualified and competed
in the two-day contest. For the first time ever in a handicapping tournament, players competed both as individuals and as members of
four-person teams representing the racetracks or race books where

they qualified. The individual winner was **Steven Walker**, a 45-year-old state environmental worker from Lincoln, Nebraska, who had qualified for the finals in a contest at Horsemen's Park. Walker won first prize of $100,000. The team competition went to the foursome from Turf Paradise, consisting of **Ken Hoskins** of Port Orchard, Washington; **Rick Leoni** of Tucson, Arizona; **Brian MacClowry** of Phoenix, Arizona; and **Steve Terelak** of Burbank, California. They earned $5,000 apiece. The event drew national media attention with coverage in *ESPN The Magazine*, and live television coverage on TVG.

OCTOBER 2000—The *National Handicapping Challenge* at the Orleans topped out with a mind-boggling 936 entries and a total purse of $518,000. That October 2000 mega-tournament was won by handicapping-contest veteran **Tim Haley** of Taylor Mill, Kentucky, who earned first prize of $163,800 after building a bankroll of $10,070 based on 12 mythical $100 win wagers per day during the three-day competition. The win was the icing on the cake of a great year for Haley, who had also won the World Championship of Race Horse Handicapping at the Club Cal-Neva in Reno in January 2000. The October 2000 National Handicapping Challenge was also notable because it was the final contest overseen by its creator, Muggsy Muniz. Muniz left Coast Resorts after 22 years of employment due, in some observers' opinions, to the company's shift away from the traditional personalized Las Vegas-style customer service that Muniz was synonymous with.

JANUARY 2001—The *DRF/NTRA National Handicapping Championship II* was held on January 12-13 at the MGM Grand in Las Vegas. The Championship was won by **Judy Wagner**, a 50-year-old retired director of a travel company from New Orleans, Louisiana. Wagner, who had qualified for the finals with a top-four finish at an earlier contest at the MGM Grand, won first prize of $100,000 for her victory over a field of 204 handicappers representing 51 tracks, OTB's, casinos, and web sites from all over North America. The Maryland Jockey Club team of **Leo Feldman** from Silver Spring, Maryland; **Gwyn Houston** from Forest Hill, Maryland; **Frank Okasaki Jr.** from Annandale, Maryland; and **Bob Ordakowski** from Hanover, Maryland, split $20,000 for winning the team competition. Wagner was awarded her title of

DRF/NTRA Handicapper of the Year two weeks later at the Eclipse Awards ceremony on January 30 in her hometown of New Orleans.

MARCH 2001—*The Suncoast Invitational* became the latest horse handicapping contest in Las Vegas. The tournament was created at the new Suncoast Resort in Las Vegas to fill the usual March time slot temporarily vacated by the National Handicapping Challenge. The $50,000 added-money contest featured a purse of $357,000 and drew a field of 307 players who paid $1,000 per entry. The inaugural Suncoast event was won by **Tommy Castillo** of Dallas, Texas, who earned a first prize of $107,450 with a contest-winning total of $10,208. Other winners of the Suncoast Invitational have included **Steve Myers** ($9,580), who earned $87,850 in January 2002, and **Ken Daniels/Robert Brendler** ($7,664), who earned $72,450 in August 2002.

MAY 2001—Penn National Racecourse announced the cancellation of the *World Series of Handicapping*, which had been in existence since 1976. Penn National claimed that increased competition from other handicapping contests, including the dozens of new DRF/NTRA National Handicapping Championship qualifying events, led to the downfall of the 24-year-old World Series of Handicapping. Only 344 people entered the event in the contest's final year, down from an average of 700 to 800 people in the contest's heyday. The winner of the final World Series, held in October 2000, was **Stephen Gaul**, a 35-year-old mechanic from Bernville, Pennsylvania.

AUGUST 2001—After a brief hiatus, the National Handicapping Challenge returned to the Orleans under its new name, *the Championship at the Orleans*. The tournament proved its staying power by drawing 663 entries for a total purse of $381,500. First place, complete with a check for $109,395, went to the father-son partnership of **Bob and Tim Downs** of Huntington Beach, California, and San Diego, California, respectively ($9,580 tournament points). The Championship at the Orleans and its newer sister contest at the Suncoast remain the biggest and most prestigious non-invitational handicapping contests in the country. The April 2002 renewal was won by **Herman Goerdon**, who earned $106,400 for finishing the contest with a total of $10,886.

JANUARY 2002—The *DRF/NTRA National Handicapping Championship III* was held at the MGM Grand race and sports book in Las Vegas on January 25-26. This time, the field was made up of 176 players representing 44 regional qualifying sites, plus defending champion Judy Wagner. The winner of the DRF/NTRA Handicapper of the Year crown was **Herman Miller**, a landscaper from Oakland, California, who had qualified for the national finals with a top-four finish in a contest held at Golden Gate Fields a month earlier. Miller won first prize of $100,000. The top team prize of $20,000 was split among Keeneland's quartet of **Richard Nilsen** from Lexington, Kentucky; **Tony Martin** from Lexington; **Don "Hee Haw" Alvey** from Louisville, Kentucky; and **Tim Holland** from Midway, Kentucky.

JUNE 2002—*The Bettor Racing OTB Midwest Classic* in Sioux Falls, South Dakota, becomes the first contest ever to bring together three DRF/NTRA National Handicapping Champions in the same event. The champs—Steven Walker of Lincoln, Nebraska (2000), Judy Wagner of New Orleans, Louisiana (2001), and Herman Miller of Oakland, California (2002)—all came from different parts of the country to compete against a star-studded field of tournament players at the remote betting outpost in South Dakota. Despite all the firepower on hand, the winner of the contest was **Donald Wright** of Eastpointe, Michigan, who earned $8,300 for the victory over a field of 83 entries. The best finish posted by the trio of national champions was 25th place, which went to Walker. Wagner finished 31st and Miller settled for 73rd place.

JANUARY 2003—The *DRF/NTRA National Handicapping Championship IV* is scheduled for Friday, January 17, and Saturday, January 18, at the race book at **Bally's Las Vegas**. The contest was moved to its new home from the MGM Grand, where it had been held during its first three years.

3

CONTEST
FORMATS

TOURNAMENTS ARE ALL about testing your horse-playing skills against your peers, but there is no single rule or format to use in order to create the truest test of handicapping ability. No two contests are created equal, and there are almost as many formats as there are contests. Therefore, it is important to understand and become familiar with all the various tournament formats in order to become a successful player.

Many of the contests on the road to the DRF/NTRA National Handicapping Championship (and many other contests, too) involve $2 to win and $2 to place wagering, or some similar variation of that common tournament format. Other varieties of this same sort of format that are equally good tests of handicapping skill include $2 across-the-board contests, and contests that simply use $2 win bets. Players all receive the same amount of bets at the start of the competition, and the ones who compile the highest earnings are declared the winners.

These straight-wagering formats involving a single horse per race are the best to use in tournament play because they are simple, straightforward, and fair to all competitors. All players start on a level playing field, and the player who earns the most money in the contest wins.

Most contests use $2 as a base amount for their wagers. This is a good amount to use for contest wagers because tote-board payoffs are calculated based on $2 wagers. However, $2 is an arbitrary amount, which just as easily could be $20, $100, or $200 based on individual preference. The base-bet amount really doesn't matter in mythical-money contests as long as the amounts are the same for everyone involved.

Besides being the best tournament format currently offered, the other main reason that the $2 win and $2 place format is becoming more and more popular is because it is the format currently being used in the National Handicapping Championship finals.

Keeping a qualifying event's format the same as the national finals helps prevent confusion while providing continuity and consistency between qualifying rounds and the finals. Tracks also want the handicappers who represent them in the national finals to do well. Sticking with the $2 to win, $2 to place format of the national finals prepares qualifying players for the national competition, and also ensures their team will be capable of excelling at the National Handicapping Championship.

Here are a few more things to remember about DRF/NTRA National Handicapping Championship qualifying contests:

- Each individual DRF/NTRA National Handicapping Championship qualifying venue is allowed to come up with its own contest, and has complete autonomy in regard to the rules, dates, duration, and format of its own event(s). Qualifying sites can come up with any sort of contest they wish, as long as they offer a total of four qualifying spots (or multiples of four) to the national championship.
- Contests can offer any amount of prize money they choose, or offer no prize money at all.
- Venues can charge entry fees of hundreds of dollars, or choose to host a free contest.
- Some contests pay back all of their entry fees in the form of prize money, while others charge a takeout in order to pay their own tournament-related expenses.
- Contests can be one-, two-, or three-day events, or even month-long or meet-long tournaments lasting a month or more.
- Some venues hold one contest offering four DRF/NTRA qualifying spots, while others hold four contests offering one DRF/NTRA qualifying spot each. Others even throw in the

kitchen sink and offer eight or 12 qualifying spots throughout the year or in a single contest.

A FEW FORMAT TWISTS . . .

There are a couple of notable contests currently doing new things with the basic $2 to win and place, or $2 across-the-board betting format, including contests such as Gulfstream Park's Turf-vivor and the annual events the Reno Hilton. Gulfstream Park and the Reno Hilton both use tournament bracket-style formats where players compete against just one player or one small group of players at a time instead of playing against the bulk of the field all at once.

It remains to be seen whether or not these types of format twists will become more widespread in the future, or if they will eventually disappear due to lack of interest. Generally speaking, it is a positive to have contest venues trying new things and getting creative with their tournament formats in an attempt to create a perfect format. However, despite being lots of fun, the contests that feature player-vs.-player matchups have not proved to be the fairest way to decide a tournament. The main flaw with bracket-style contests is that players with lower scores can advance and win over players with higher scores. This sort of outcome goes against everything that handicapping tournaments are based on, and therefore are avoided by many players who see these formats as unfair.

For example, assume a brackets-style contest features matchups of Player A vs. Player B, and Player C vs. Player D. Player A could defeat Player B by a score of $100 to $80, while Player C beats Player D by a score of $60 to $50. In this case, Player A ($100) advances to face Player C ($60) despite the fact that Player B outscored Player C by $20. Player B loses, and Player C then gets a chance to beat Player A even though Player C had only the third-best score out of the above four players.

Clearly, under this type of format, the best player doesn't always win. Low-scoring players can beat higher-scoring players, and that doesn't add up to the best and fairest contest format out there today.

WIDER SELECTION IS BETTER

One of the biggest ways in which tournaments differ from one another is in the number of tracks that they include in their betting menu. Ideally,

HANDICAPPING CONTEST HANDBOOK

a contest should offer full cards from as many different tracks as possible to give players a wide variety of races to choose from. More tracks mean more chances for handicappers to zero in on more best-bet selections, more overlays, and more kinds of races from around the country.

The National Handicapping Championship attracts players from all over the country and therefore includes races from at least eight different tracks encompassing several regions and race circuits. Many other major tournaments routinely offer five to six different tracks, which is also a nice selection. Six or eight tracks is good when you can get it, but a tournament format can still be good with as few as three, or even two, different tracks.

While more definitely is better, there are many contests that offer races from just one track on their betting menu. In some cases, tracks are prohibited from offering out-of-state simulcasts or limited to a certain number of such races, and in other cases, tracks simply choose to highlight their own product.

In one-track tournaments, players are usually betting all the same races as everyone else. In multi-track events, players have a choice of what races to play. It's nice to have everyone in a contest focusing on the same races at the same time from an excitement standpoint, but having a choice is always better than having none. There are other, better ways of building excitement during a contest besides limiting the contest to races from only one racetrack.

MANDATORY RACES

One of the great moments in any handicapping tournament is when the crowd erupts in noise and cheering as an important contest race is being run. This element of energy is always present in one-track tournaments where everyone is playing the same races, but unfortunately it's not always a part of multi-track contests where the bets are scattered around on so many different races and tracks simultaneously.

Thanks to the idea of mandatory races, however, tournaments have found a way to offer a wide variety of tracks, while still making energy and noise into a big part of what a contest is all about.

Mandatory races are races that every player in a contest must bet. They are picked out in advance by the tournament organizers and usually represent a wide variety of different class levels, surfaces, and distances akin to a sort of handicapping obstacle course. Mandatory races can be a small part of a handicapping contest, or they can represent as many as half of a contest's overall plays.

An ideal contest format should offer multiple tracks, and include both mandatory and optional races. This way, the field has the freedom to go separate ways during a contest, but still must come back together at least a few times a day when the mandatory races are being run.

REAL MONEY VS. MYTHICAL MONEY

Most people will agree that the best tournament formats are not only the ones that are the most simple and straightforward, but also the ones that best cut down the unavoidable element of luck that is involved in all kinds of horse handicapping contests.

There are those who argue that no tournament format can truly be fair unless it utilizes a real-money betting format as opposed to mythical money. It is hard to argue with this way of thinking considering that we bet real money—not mythical money—every single day we bet on horse racing. Betting, after all, is what the sport of horse racing revolves around, and therefore it is a good idea to have some form of real-money wagering involved in a contest whenever possible.

Real-money contests aren't as prevalent as they once were, but they're still out there and are a nice change of pace when you can find them.

Real-money contests often follow the same format as mythical-money contests with the added dimension that you keep whatever funds remain in your bankroll at the conclusion. Some players like real-money contests because the results in these events are more realistic. The idea is that players are more hesitant to play crazy longshots when real-money gains and losses are on the line. Real-money contests also favor their hosts by adding actual additional handle instead of "mythical" handle, which really isn't handle at all.

Not all real-money tournaments are necessarily a good thing, however. Some real-money tournaments turn what are intended to be handicapping contests into betting contests.

There are two kinds of real-money contests. First, there are open-bankroll "reality" events where you bet freely, just as you would on a normal day at the track. Players may bet and re-bet their money on any type of wager, including exotics, and the one who comes up with the highest total at the end of the day is the winner. The second kind of real-money contest we're seeing is a traditional $2 to win, $2 to place type of contest format where the bets are made with real money instead of mythical money.

Everyone has his own preferences, of course, but I believe that reality contests are not really handicapping contests at all. Reality-style real-money contests are just like a normal day at the track, but if people wanted a normal day at the track then they would go to the track and not play in contests. Most tournament players enter contests for something different from their normal racetrack experience, and that's why these contests have not increased in popularity.

The type of real-money contest that is gaining in popularity, however, is the second kind of real-money contest—the kind that uses a traditional tournament format with real-money bets instead of mythical money. These contests are an excellent idea, because they put real money through the mutuels (a benefit for contest hosts) while still maintaining the credibility of the traditional tournament formats.

Real-money betting has an uncanny way of removing an element of blind longshot-stabbing from contests, which is a major turnoff for many would-be players. People are not as free-wheeling when it's real money they're losing instead of mythical money. It doesn't matter if a contest format is $2 to win and place, or even $20 to win and place—real-money bets can help keep contestants honest, and therefore reduce the element of luck that has always existed in handicapping contests.

LUCK—IT'S A FOUR-LETTER WORD

One of the best things and one of the worst things about handicapping contests is that anything can happen. You must learn to expect the unexpected, and this single fact is the reason why so many people love contests, and so many others loathe them. If you ever have played, or ever will play in handicapping contests, you know that you will eventually see a little bit of everything under the sun.

A contest winner does not necessarily need to be the best handicapper in the world. Instead, contest winners are often just the people who perform the best within the limited confines of a particular contest, or the ones who best understand how to take advantage of a contest's wagering framework. The perfect format for a handicapping contest has yet to be devised and probably never will be. Therefore, you must face the fact that luck will eventually enter into this game.

Handicapping tournaments are not really designed to be long-range measurements of a person's overall handicapping ability. Instead, they are short-term races to the highest bankroll over a brief, specific period of time. A tournament win is certainly a feather in the cap of any handicapper, but true handicapping prowess is more accurately measured over the sum of a player's contest career, not through a win or loss in a single contest.

Some longtime handicappers are turned off by the role luck can play in some contests. However, luck is no more a part of the game of handicapping tournaments than it is a part of the game of Thoroughbred racing as a whole. If you've already accepted the fact that the best horse in a race doesn't always win, it's not a far leap to accept that the best handicapper in a contest doesn't always win. Luck is a huge part of racing, and luck is a huge part of handicapping contests. Deal with it, accept it, enjoy it, and move on in spite of it. Luck is an unavoidable part of the world of handicapping contests, and you shouldn't let the role luck can play ruin your fun.

THE TALE OF AUDREY LOUIE-SELLERS

One of the best stories ever to emerge from a handicapping contest is the tale of Audrey Louie-Sellers, who, in February 2000, turned the Flamingo Reno Winter Challenge into one of the strangest and most amazing handicapping tournaments ever held.

A field of 270 handicappers assembled in Reno for that infamous contest that is now well known in the annals of tournament lore. At the time, the twice-annual Flamingo Reno Challenges were among the biggest and most popular contests in the country, with prize money in the neighborhood of $150,000 routinely luring some of the most prominent tournament players from across the nation.

In February 2000, however, despite the usual star-studded Flamingo Reno field of tourney veterans and professional handicappers, Audrey Louie-Sellers, a total novice, took home a first-place check for $56,855.

This contest was more than just a case of David beating Goliath. Louie-Sellers wasn't just a novice. She didn't know how to handicap or bet, and hadn't even planned to be at the contest that week.

Louie-Sellers was a restaurant/nightclub owner from 3,000 miles away in Durham, North Carolina. She claimed she didn't gamble and hadn't been to a racetrack once since the 1970's. She had traveled to Oakland, California, to visit her brother, George Louie, who was an avid tournament player and Flamingo Reno regular who had already entered the February contest in advance. George decided to bring Audrey with him from Oakland to Reno primarily to act as a baby-sitter for his young son. In the process, George also agreed to put up an extra $500 entry fee in order to give Audrey an opportunity to pass some time and play in the contest.

The baby-sitting investment paid off, and then some. Louie-Sellers not only won the contest but also set an all-time Flamingo Reno Challenge record with a final tournament total of $22,945 based on 10 mythical $100 across-the-board bets a day during the three-day, 30-race contest ($9,000 original bankroll).

After nearly forgetting to hand in her 10 contest plays, Louie-Sellers totaled $3,435 on Day One of the contest and then went on an unimaginable streak on Day Two, when she earned an enormous daily total of $15,940, quintupling her $3,000 daily bankroll. Those winnings gave Louie-Sellers an almost insurmountable total for the entire contest. Of her 10 across-the-board bets on that lucky day, Louie-Sellers posted seven winners and almost all were longshots. Louie-Sellers added to her bankroll on the contest's final day to finish at $22,945, which was more than $3,000 ahead of her nearest competitors, runner-up Murray Cram, a handicapping software developer and avid bettor from California, and third-place finisher Ira Schwartz, a professional handicapper from Florida.

The Cinderella story was something of a fairy tale for Louie-Sellers, but certainly not everyone at the Flamingo Reno was amused. Cram and Schwartz, who have won and lost thousands of dollars playing in too many tournaments to remember, were not laughing. Still, both understood that it is part of the game in the world of handicapping contests, and neither begrudged the winner her victory.

Louie-Sellers later recalled, "I don't know anything about horse racing. I don't know anything about the odds, and I don't know anything about [*Daily Racing Form*]. I picked up some sheets with the horses' names on it [overnights] and I bet the ones with the names I liked. There was also one jockey who I kept betting because we have the same name, [Shane] Sellers."

The tale of Audrey Louie-Sellers is more the exception than the rule when it comes to tournaments. Still, this story and others like it are part of the reason why tournaments so readily capture the imagination of horseplayers. Luck and longshots can work against you, but they can also work with you and turn you into a champion.

When it comes to contests, one nice longshot or a well-timed hot streak is often all it takes to turn an also-ran into a grand-prize winner.

ODDS CAPS

There are many ways that luck can be limited in handicapping contests. One of the most important ways to ensure a fair contest is to install an odds cap on all winning payoffs. Odds caps for win horses are usually either 20-1 ($42) or 25-1 ($52). Place payoffs are normally capped at 10-1 ($22), 12-1 ($26), or 15-1 ($32), and show payoffs, when used, are usually capped at 5-1 ($10).

Odds caps are always a good idea in tournaments, because they prevent people who are out of contention from stabbing at 100-1 horses that can move them from the cellar to the penthouse all at once by sheer luck. These 100-1 horses aren't supposed to win very often in horse racing, but they always seem to win during contests. When they do win, and there is no odds cap, they inevitably change the complexion of a whole tournament from a test of skill to a matter of luck.

Contests should not be won with a single horse, and the installation of odds caps can usually prevent that from happening.

There are still many contests around the country that do not have odds caps. Playing in these events is like playing Russian roulette. A competitor can outplay and out-handicap the rest of the field for an entire contest only to lose to 10 longshot-stabbing cellar-dwellers whose only chance to win crosses the finish line first at 100-1 in the final race of the day. And there's no faster way to turn someone off to handicapping contests than when a lucky 100-1 horse ends up deciding a tournament.

ANATOMY OF A $213.80 HORSE

Anyone who ever wondered why handicapping tournaments need odds caps need look no farther than the inaugural Sports Haven Handicapping Challenge, which was held February 1-2, 1997, in New Haven, Connecticut.

The brand-new two-day contest's rules did not include an odds cap, and that fact was not lost on handicappers from the very beginning of the event. On the contest's first day, several players distanced themselves from the field when 54-1 shot Criminal Suit won the day's 11th race at Gulfstream and returned $110.80. This horse, and the entrants who cashed on him, changed the entire dynamic of the tournament from a competitive test of handicapping ability to a scavenger hunt for the highest-priced horses left in the contest. Horseplayers became stabbers looking exclusively for 50-1 or 100-1 horses, because they were the only ones they could play if they hoped to have a chance.

During the second and final day of the contest, some legitimate players began to move themselves back into the standings, but most others fell far out of contention. The tournament had basically turned into a free-for-all just in time for the running of Gulfstream Park's 10th race, the Hutcheson Stakes, a sprint for 3-year-olds going seven furlongs.

The stars of that year's Hutcheson were supposed to be Confide, who was exiting a Grade 3 win in the six-furlong Spectacular Bid Stakes at Gulfstream, and Ordway, a colt coming off a layoff after winning the Champagne Stakes and finishing third in the Breeders' Cup Juvenile the previous fall. One favorite was stretching out, the other was cutting back. The race drew a total of eight horses, and the lowest Beyer Speed Figure in the bunch belonged to Frisk Me Now, who was coming out of a third-place finish in a strong seven-furlong Gulfstream allowance two weeks before.

Frisk Me Now had some handicapping angles in his favor, including the fact that he had showed improved early speed in his last race despite breaking slowly near the back of an 11-horse field. Frisk Me Now's primary appeal, however, at least to players in this particular contest, was the fact that he had drifted up to 99-1 on the tote board by post time of the race.

The rest, as they say, is history. Ordway was waiting to be stretched out and used the Hutcheson as a prep. Confide got hooked in a suicidal speed duel with Crown Ambassador, and none other than Frisk Me Now came rumbling down the center of the track to win in 1:22.20.

Frisk Me Now's final odds were 105-1, and 19 players in the 281-person Sports Haven field had placed the maximum wager on him in the contest. Those 19 players finished in the top 19 places in the contest, which paid off to its top 20 finishers. Either you won that race, or you lost the contest.

The result of the 1997 Hutcheson Stakes led to the installation of an odds cap at all subsequent Sports Haven tournaments, and still serves as a valuable lesson as to why handicapping contests need to have odds caps in order to be regarded as fair and prestigious events.

1 Hoop Coyote Hoop

Own: Double N Stables (—) 1996:(429 61 .14)

B. c. 3 (Mar)
Sire: Once Wild (Baldski)
Dam: Lady Jet Setter (Noble Table)
Br: Stodghill Jason J (Fla)
Tr: Rera Cathleen J(1 0 0 0 .00) 96:(62 17 .27)

119

Lifetime Record:	6	3	1	0	$91,962
1997	1	1	0	0	$1,296	Turf	0 0 0 0
1996	5	3	0	0	$90,666	Wet	1 1 0 0	$24,000
GP	0	0	0	0		Dist	1 0 1 0	$1,296

KLINKE W S (—) 1996:(429 61 .14)

2 President's Decree

Own: Little Fish Stable Inc

Dk. b or br c. 3 (Mar)
Sire: Capote (Seattle Slew)
Dam: Mitterand (Hold Your Peace)
Br: Irving Cowan & Marjorie Cowan (Ky)
Tr: Walden W Elliett(11 2 3 0 .18) 96:(396 62 .17)

L 114

Lifetime Record:	2	1	1	0	$27,420
1997	1	0	1	0	$5,510	Turf	0 0 0 0
1996	1	1	0	0	$21,910	Wet	0 0 0 0
GP	1	0	1	0	$5,510	Dist	0 0 0 0

SELLERS S J (161 32 27 26 .20) 1996:(329 207 .22)

3 Y'All Can

Own: Rosuer Stables Inc

Dk. b or br c. 3 (Mar)
Sire: With Approval (Caro*Ire)
Dam: Fence Stretcher (Native Roman)
Br: Scott W R (Fla)
Tr: Zito Nicholas P(30 7 7 2 .23) 96:(400 62 .16)

L 114

Lifetime Record:	5	2	2	0	$46,210
1996	5	2	2	0	$46,210	Turf	0 0 0 0
1995	0	M	0	0		Wet	0 0 0 0
GP						Dist	0 0 0 0

KARAMANOS H A (2 0 0 0 .00) (—)

4 Frisk Me Now

Own: Dender Carol R
KING E L JR (42 2 4 6 .05) 1996:(782 98 .13)

B. c. 3 (May)
Sire: Mister Frisky (Marsayas)
Dam: Slew Me Now (Tsunami Slew)
Br: Farnsworth Farms (Fla)
Tr: Durso Robert J(19 1 2 4 .05) 96:(197 26 .13)

112

Lifetime Record: 7 1 1 4 $26,695
1997 1 0 0 1 $2,900 | Turf 0 0 0 0
1996 6 1 1 3 $23,795 | Wet 1 0 1 0 $4,000
GP 1 0 0 1 $2,900 | Dist 1 0 0 1 $2,900

18Jan97-9GP fst 7f :22^{2} :46 1:11^{1} 1:24^{1} Alw 29000N1X 79 3 9 3½ 1½ 3½ 3¾ King E L Jr 117 30.30 80-17 Tansit117¾ Zede1172½ Frisk Me Now1178½ Weakened 3 path 11
26Dec96-8Crc fst 1 :23^{2} :47^{1} 1:13^{2} 1:40^{3} Alw 25500N1X 67 4 4 44½ 54½ 47½ 3^{11} King E L Jr 117 5.20 73-27 Gold Book1206½ Telesham1174½ Frisk Me Now117hd Some early foot 10
10Dec96-9Crc fst 6f :21^{4} :45^{2} :58^{2} 1:11^{4} Alw 22500N1X 79 3 5 76 58½ 45 34 King E L Jr 117 3.10 84-19 Tureen Of Gold1173½ Premiere Cherokee112½ Frisk Me Now1172½ 9
Steadied early, 5-wide, mild rally
22Nov96-7Med fst 6f :22^{3} :46 :58^{2} 1:12 Alw 20000N1X 68 6 6 53½ 53½ 34½ 32½ King E L Jr 118 *1.90 77-22 Pappy's Halo116nk Christian Soldier1162 Frisk Me Now1187¾ Mild bid 6
10Aug96-6Mth fst 6f :22^{1} :46 :58^{3} 1:11^{3} Md Sp Wt 73 7 7 42 2½ 1hd 12½ King E L Jr 118 3.20 85-17 Frisk Me Now1182½ Time To Gamble1183½ Real Star1184½ Driving 11
26Jly96-11Mth sly 5½f :22 :45^{1} :57^{4} 1:04^{2} Md Sp Wt 70 6 1 33½ 34½ 35 25½ King E L Jr 118 4.40 92-10 Harley Tune1185½ Frisk Me Now1181 Gables1186½ Earned place 7
12Jly96-5Mth fst 5½f :22^{3} :46^{1} :58^{4} 1:05^{2} Md Sp Wt 60 6 3 42½ 53½ 44½ 44 King E L Jr 118 5.90 88-15 Just A Cat1183½ Gables118no Sal's Driver118¾ Some late gain 7

WORKOUTS: Jan30 GP 4f fst :48^{2} H 10/34 Jan15 GP 4f sly :49^{3} H (d) 7/15 Dec21 GP 5f fst 1:01 H 2/35 Dec4 GP 4f fst :48 H 2/17 Nov20 Med 3f fst :35^{1} Hg 3/16 Nov13 Med 7f fst 1:27^{4} B 1/2

5 Crown Ambassador

Own: Anstu Stable & Hart–Pletcher Stable
DAY P (98 15 14 10 .15) 1996:(1339 272 .20)

Ch. c. 3 (Apr)
Sire: Storm Cat (Storm Bird)
Dam: Rare Mint (Key to the Mint)
Br: Flaxman Holdings Ltd (Ky)
Tr: Pletcher Todd A(17 2 2 7 .12) 96:(206 33 .16)

L 117

Lifetime Record: 7 2 0 2 $75,446
1997 1 0 0 1 $8,250 | Turf 0 0 0 0
1996 6 2 0 1 $67,196 | Wet 1 0 0 0 $12,000
GP 1 0 0 1 $8,250 | Dist 0 0 0 0

5Jan97-10GP fst 6f :21^{2} :43^{2} :56^{2} 1:09^{4} SpectclrBid-G3 79 7 3 4½ 21 33½ 35½ Velazquez J R L 117 b 10.60 86-11 Confide1143¾ Kelly Kip1191½ Crown Ambassador117¾ Weakened 9
1Dec96-8Aqu sly 1⅛ :48^{2} 1:13 1:39^{4} 1:53^{2} Remsen-G2 80 2 1 11½ 12 32 47 Luzzi M J L 114 b 14.60 66-24 The Silver Move1144½ Jules1222½ Accelerator122hd Speed weakened 8
2Nov96-8CD fst 1 :22^{4} :46 1:10^{4} 1:36^{2} Iroquois-G3 82 3 2 31 2hd 42½ 57½ Martinez W L 114 b 3.20 83-17 Global View112½ Partner's Hero1124 Haint121hd Dueled, tired 6
5Oct96-4Kee fst 6½f :22^{1} :45^{2} 1:10^{2} 1:16^{3} Alw 38660N2L 90 3 4 11 11½ 14 17½ Martinez W L 122 b 5.40 92-14 CrownAmbssdor1227½ TrumnC.1221½ WesternGmblr1163½ Pace, ridden out 8
11Sep96-7TP fst 5½f :22^{3} :46^{1} :58^{3} 1:05 Md Sp Wt 79 5 2 12 12 14 14½ Martinez W L 121 b 2.40 — — Crown Ambassador1214½ Rojo Dinero1211 Lasting Approval1218 12
Bore in bumped start, pace, ridden out
29Jly96-2Sar fst 6f :22^{2} :46^{2} :58^{4} 1:11^{2} Md Sp Wt 70 6 3 11 11 1½ 33 Santos J A 119 b 8.90 81-12 Haint1191 Snow Birdie1192 Crown Ambassador1195½ Speed, weakened 12
23Jun96-4Bel fst 5f :22^{2} :45^{2} :57^{4} Md Sp Wt 50 1 3 31½ 2hd 45 610½ Bailey J D 117 *1.40 86-05 Rapid Robyn1174 Smoke Signal117nk Big Friendly117½ Speed, tired 8

WORKOUTS: Jan20 GP 5f fst 1:01^{3} H 12/19 Dec30 GP 4f fst :50^{1} H 23/29 Dec17 GP 4f fst :51 B 44/52 Nov20 Bel 6f fst 1:15 H 4/4 Nov13 Bel 4f fst :48^{2} H 10/41

6 Confide

Own: New Farm
SMITH M E (108 16 13 8 .15) 1996:(1416 254 .18)

B. c. 3 (May)
Sire: Phone Trick (Clever Trick)
Dam: Bag of Tricks (Devil's Bag)
Br: Greely John J III (Ky)
Tr: Perkins Benjamin W(15 3 4 3 .20) 96:(174 58 .33)

L 117

Lifetime Record: 6 3 3 0 $104,326
1997 1 1 0 0 $45,000 | Turf 0 0 0 0
1996 5 2 3 0 $59,326 | Wet 1 1 0 0 $12,000
GP 1 1 0 0 $45,000 | Dist 0 0 0 0

5Jan97-10GP fst 6f :21^{2} :43^{2} :56^{2} 1:09^{4} SpectclrBid-G3 93 5 7 3nk 31 12 13¾ Smith M E L 114 b 2.40 91-11 Confide1143¾ Kelly Kip1191½ Crown Ambassador117¾ Driving inside
27Nov96-8Aqu fst 6f :22^{2} :46^{2} :59^{1} 1:12^{3} Huntington54k 87 4 3 31½ 31 21 22 Bravo J L 117 b 1.90 78-25 Kelly Kip1222 Confide1173½ Oro Bandito114¾ Bid, 2nd best
14Oct96-9Lrl fst 6f :21^{4} :44^{4} :57^{1} 1:10^{1} Bimelech31k 89 4 7 21½ 2½ 12 2no Wilson R 115 *.70 92-16 Captain Bodgit119no Confide1153 Well Challenged115hd Lugged in 1/8
21Sep96-2TP fst 6f :21^{2} :44^{2} :57 1:10 Alw 37600N$Y 83 4 1 11½ 12½ 15 13 Smith M E 115 *.30 93-10 Confide1153 Leestown1213½ St. Cloud1186 Pace, driving
30Jun96-2Mth sly 5½f :21^{4} :45^{1} :58^{2} 1:05^{2} Md Sp Wt 83 2 2 2hd 2½ 1hd 1½ Bravo J 118 *.30 92-12 Confide118½ Smoke Glacken1184½ Capture The Gold1185 Driving, rail
9Jun96-3Bel fst 5f :22 :45^{1} :57^{4} Md Sp Wt 90 3 1 1hd 1hd 1½ 21 Smith M E 115 *.50 96-15 Zede1151 Confide1152 Rapid Robyn1153½ Dueled, couldn't last

WORKOUTS: Jan29 GP 5f fst :59 H 2/32 ●Jan23 GP 6f fst 1:12 B 1/8 ●Jan17 GP 5f fst 1:00 H 1/59 ●Jan1 GP 3f fst :35^{4} B 1/12 Dec26 GP 5f fst :59^{1} H 5/11 Dec20 GP 4f fst :48 H 4/39

7 Time to Gamble
Own: King Roger
BRAVO J (105 14 19 13 .13) 1996:(1140 243 .21)

Gr/ro c. 3 (Jan)
Sire: Prospectors Gamble (Crafty Prospector)
Dam: No Time to Play (Buck Private)
Br: Hart Mr & Mrs E C (Fla)
Tr: Hine Hubert(16 1 3 1 .06) 96:(144 27 .19)

L 112

Lifetime Record : 4 2 2 0 $43,135
1996 4 2 2 0 $43,135 Turf 0 0 0 0
1995 0 M 0 0 Wet 1 1 0 0 $13,200
GP 0 0 0 0 Dist 0 0 0 0

23Oct96-4Kee gd 6f :22 :454 :582 1:114 Alw 34448N2L 90 5 1 11½ 11½ 12½ 11½ Sellers S J 116 *1.10 79-19 TimeToGamble1161½ WesternGambler1161 NorthSlem1162½ Pace, driving 6
13Oct96-6Kee fst 6f :214 :454 :582 1:111 Alw 39128N2L 88 6 2 21½ 21 1hd 2hd Sellers S J 116 *.90 82-20 Mr.Gumbo116hd TimeToGmble1161 NorthSlem1162 Bid, led, outfinished 6
24Aug96-1Mth my 6f :222 :462 :582 1:111 Md Sp Wt 67 7 1 11½ 12½ 11½ 14¾ Bravo J 118 *.40 87-12 Time To Gamble1184¾ Open Election1182¼ Concerto1182 Ridden out 7
10Aug96-6Mth fst 6f :221 :46 :583 1:113 Md Sp Wt 67 4 5 11 1½ 2hd 22¼ Bravo J 118 *.70 83-17 Frisk Me Now1182¼ Time To Gamble1183½ Real Star1184½ 2nd best 11
WORKOUTS: Jan31 GP 3f fst :354 B 3/15 ●Jan24 GP 5f fst :59 Hg 1/40 Jan17 GP 6f fst 1:14 H 2/10 Jan11 GP 5f fst 1:012 H 11/32 ●Jan4 GP 4f fst :462 H 1/46 Dec29 GP 5f fst 1:003 H 5/30

8 Ordway
Own: Dileo Philip F & Punk William
VELAZQUEZ J R (118 16 13 17 .14) 1996:(1363 212 .16)

Dk. b or br c. 3 (Mar)
Sire: Salt Lake (Deputy Minister)
Dam: Priceless Countess (Vaguely Noble*GB)
Br: Lantern Hill Farm (Ky)
Tr: Donk David(10 2 1 1 .20) 96:(201 41 .20)

119

Lifetime Record : 5 2 2 1 $426,700
1996 5 2 2 1 $426,700 Turf 0 0 0 0
1995 0 M 0 0 Wet 0 0 0 0
GP 0 0 0 0 Dist 1 0 1 0 $40,000

26Oct96-8WO fst 1 1/16 :231 :464 1:11 1:432 B C Juv-G1 94 6 8 74½ 77 44½ 32¾ Velazquez J R 122 *1.40 89-02 Boston Harbor122nk Acceptable1222½ Ordway1222½ 10
Blocked far turn, split horses, rallied
5Oct96-9Bel fst 1 1/16 :23 :46 1:103 1:42 Champagne-G1 101 1 7 62¾ 62¾ 31 11¾ Velazquez J R 122 7.50 89-10 Ordway1221¾ Traitor1222 Gold Tribute1222¼ 12
Blocked turn, split horses 1/8 pl, clear
31Aug96-8Sar fst 7f :213 :441 1:093 1:233 Hopeful-G1 74 8 4 64½ 53½ 25 29 Velazquez J R 122 4.00 79-12 Smoke Glacken1229 Ordway1222 Gun Fight122¾ No match, clear 2nd 8
12Aug96-2Sar fst 6½f :22 :454 1:101 1:162 Md Sp Wt 91 2 3 31½ 52½ 2hd 12¼ Velazquez J R 119 *1.40 93-10 Ordway1192¼ Copper Canyon1195 Smoke Signal1191½ 10
Checked 1/2 pl, awaited room turn
18Jly96-6Bel fst 6f :223 :46 :58 1:103 Md Sp Wt 80 11 10 64½ 21 2hd 2nk Velazquez J R 116 5.00 89-11 Mercer Mill116nk Ordway1165 Khalsa116¾ Broke slow, five wide 12
WORKOUTS: Jan30 GP 4f fst :503 B 28/34 Jan24 GP 5f fst :593 H 2/40 Jan18 GP 6f fst 1:14 Bg 2/22 ●Jan7 GP 6f fst 1:14 H 1/6 ●Jan1 GP 5f fst 1:004 H 1/11 Dec28 GP 5f fst 1:043 B 36/39

TENTH RACE

Gulfstream

FEBRUARY 2, 1997

7 FURLONGS. (1.20³) **44th Running of THE DANKA HUTCHESON. (Third Leg of The Florida Derby Series). Purse $100,000 guaranteed. Grade II. 3-year-olds. By subscription of $100 each which shall accompany the nomination, $1,000 to pass the entry box and $1,000 additional to start, with $100,000 guaranteed. The owner of the winner to receive $60,000, $20,000 to second, $11,000 to third, $6,000 to fourth, $3,000 to fifth. Weight, 122 lbs. Non-winners of $50,000 twice, allowed 3 lbs. $50,000 or $30,000 in 1996, 5 lbs. $25,000, 8 lbs. $20,000 or two races other than maiden or claiming, 10 lbs. Starters to be named through the entry box by the usual time of closing. Horses finishing, first, second, or third in the Danka Hutcheson Stakes will automatically be nominated to the Florida Derby. Trophy to winning owner. This race will be limited to 14 starters, with also eligibles. (High weights preferred.) Closed Wednesday, January 22 with 141 early nominations and 7 late nominations, total of 148.**

Value of Race: $100,000 Winner $60,000; second $20,000; third $11,000; fourth $6,000; fifth $3,000. Mutuel Pool $586,248.00 Exacta Pool $466,727.00 Trifecta Pool $383,689.00

Last Raced	Horse	M/Eqt.	A.	Wt	PP	St	¼	½	Str	Fin	Jockey	Odds $1
18Jan97 9GP³	Frisk Me Now		3	112	4	4	6½	4hd	3¹¹	1¾	King E L Jr	105.90
5Jan97 10GP¹	Confide	Lb	3	117	6	2	1½	1hd	1hd	2½	Smith M E	1.50
5Jan97 10GP³	Crown Ambassador	Lb	3	117	5	6	2¹	2³	2¹½	3⅜	Day P	13.30
8Jan97 7GP²	President's Decree	L	3	114	2	5	3hd	3hd	4⁷	4¹⁰	Sellers S J	3.50
14Jan97 9Tam²	Hoop Coyote Hoop		3	119	1	7	7³	7hd	5³	5⁶	Klinke W S	25.70
23Oct96 4Kee¹	Time to Gamble	L	3	112	7	1	4hd	5hd	7¹	6½	Bravo J	8.20
11Aug96 11Crc⁹	Y'All Can	L	3	118	3	8	5½	6²½	6²½	7hd	Karamanos H A	63.30
26Oct96 8WO³	Ordway		3	119	8	3	8	8	8	8	Velazquez J R	1.80

OFF AT 5:13 Start Good. Won driving. Time, :21⁴, :44², 1:09¹, 1:22² Track fast.

$2 Mutuel Prices:

4–FRISK ME NOW	213.80	39.20	8.20
6–CONFIDE		3.80	2.60
5–CROWN AMBASSADOR			4.20

$2 EXACTA 4 & 6 PAID $666.00 $2 TRIFECTA 4-6-5 PAID $3,967.20

B. c, (May), by Mister Frisky–Slew Me Now, by Tsunami Slew. Trainer Durso Robert J. Bred by Farnsworth Farms (Fla).

FRISK ME NOW reserved early, bumped leaving the backstretch when Y'ALL CAN tried to get out, came into the stretch in the four path, then under right handed urging outfinished CONFIDE. The latter sprinted to a slim lead, set the pace while under pressure from CROWN AMBASSADOR, but could not match strides with the winner and held on gamely for the place in the three path. CROWN AMBASSADOR vied for the lead from the beginning then weakened in the drive. PRESIDENT'S DECREE a forward factor in the beginning then lacked the needed late response. HOOP COYOTE HOOP void of early foot, then made a mild late bid. TIME TO GAMBLE within striking distance early then faded. Y'ALL CAN away slowly, tried to get out leaving the backstretch bumped FRISK ME NOW then gave way. ORDWAY was no factor wide in the stretch.

Owners— 1, Dender Carol R; 2, New Farm; 3, Anstu Stable & Hart-Pletcher Stable; 4, Little Fish Stable Inc; 5, Double N Stables; 6, King Roger; 7, Rosuer Stables Inc; 8, Dileo Philip F & Punk William

Trainers— 1, Durso Robert J; 2, Perkins Benjamin W; 3, Pletcher Todd A; 4, Walden W Elliott; 5, Rera Cathleen J; 6, Hine Hubert; 7, Zito Nicholas P; 8, Donk David

Overweight: Y'All Can (4).

SCOREBOARD OR NO SCOREBOARD, THAT IS THE QUESTION

One of the biggest arguments existing among tournament players doesn't have anything to do with what format is the best, or if mythical-money or real-money betting should be used. The most heated debate, by far, exists over the issue of whether or not tournaments should provide score postings, or scoreboards, to update players on their positions throughout the duration of a contest.

My feeling on this debate is that scoreboards add to the enjoyment of a handicapping tournament by adding to the overall competitive atmosphere of the event. After all, players and teams in most sports know exactly where they stand at all points during a game in terms of the score and the time remaining. The question is whether scores are relevant at all points during a horse handicapping contest, and whether posting scores can affect the integrity of the results.

Jeff Sotman and John Curran, two industry professionals who are also tournament enthusiasts, hold opposite viewpoints on this hot-button issue facing handicapping tournaments.

Sotman, the tournament director for the DRF/NTRA National Handicapping Championship and general manager of *The Horseplayer Magazine,* strongly believes that scoreboards should not be used in handicapping contests.

"Posting results at every point in time makes no sense to me, because scores at interim periods throughout a tournament are completely irrelevant," he contends. "Except for contests where every entrant plays exactly the same races, there is only downside and no upside in posting scores. When scores are posted at arbitrary times during a tournament, the comparisons between players are purely apples to oranges because there are almost no players who have made the exact same amount of plays at any given point. In some extreme examples, some players may be all done with their contest plays [East Coast races] at a point in time when other players have not even started yet [West Coast races].

"Additionally, posting scores is a clear penalty against a contest's strongest players—the leaders. If the goal of a handicapping tournament is to reward the best player(s), giving everyone in the field a target score to shoot for clearly works against this goal and is a crime against the leader who must pray that something wacky doesn't happen to steal the win from him.

"Finally, in my opinion, scoreboards don't increase strategy, but rather, they reduce strategy in tournament play. When the scores of the leaders are posted, it makes it perfectly clear what everyone behind the leader should do in order to win."

Curran, the track announcer and race caller at Delaware Park, and a former DRF/NTRA National Handicapping Championship qualifier, takes the opposite viewpoint that scoreboards are part of what makes tournaments great.

"Part of the fun of being in a contest is knowing where you stand and figuring out your next move," he says. "Strategy is a wonderful part of any event. When you're shooting for prizes up to $100,000, not knowing where you stand going into the last few races of a contest is like hiding the clock in the last two minutes of a football game. 'Oh, you say you scored? Well I'm sorry, but the game ended 30 seconds ago and you lost!'

"When I was in college I frequently corresponded with sportscaster Curt Gowdy, and I'll never forget one of the things he always said. 'You can never give the score and time often enough,' because, as he explained, 'everything that happens depends on what the score is and how much time is left.' A running play up the middle in a football game by a team protecting a 14-point lead late in the fourth quarter would be a good play call, but the same play when down 14 points in the fourth quarter would not be a good play call.

"That's why I think it's so important to keep players in handicapping tournaments updated on where they stand as soon as possible and as often as possible. Strategy is a great part of a contest, and playing in the dark in terms of scores takes a great deal of fun out of it."

Both Curran and Sotman present effective arguments for the opposite sides of this issue. Sotman makes a good point in saying that scores are largely irrelevant when different players in the same contest are playing different races. In my opinion, however, the stance that score-posting penalizes the leaders doesn't hold water, given that scoreboards are used in almost all other forms of competition. Try telling Tiger Woods he's not allowed to know how many strokes ahead or behind he is on the final day of a golf tournament. It just won't work.

As a matter of fact, one of the only sports that doesn't show the score is boxing, and if anything, boxing could benefit, at least in terms of integrity, if judges' scorecards were posted.

You can argue whether scoreboards add to or detract from strategy. But it is difficult to argue that scoreboards, when done properly, add to the fun, excitement, and overall atmosphere of a handicapping contest. They must be done right, however, for them to be a truly good idea at any tournament.

The best examples of scoreboards are those used in the Autotote tournaments at Sports Haven and the Bradley Teletheater in Connecticut, and at the New York Racing Association's contests at Belmont Park and Aqueduct. The reason these scoreboards are done well is because they not only update scores constantly, but also update the number of bets a player has made and how many he has remaining. It's like Curt Gowdy said, you can never show the score and the time—in this case, the number of bets remaining—often enough.

Scores at any arbitrary time in a contest are irrelevant unless they are also accompanied by a count of how many bets a player has made up to that point. If scores can be displayed in this way, they can only add to a contest's appeal and should be posted for all to see as often as possible.

4

STRATEGY

YOU CAN'T GO into a contest without a game plan, so now that you're familiar with the different types of tournaments, you can start focusing on strategies and finding the best way to win.

As discussed in the last chapter, most contests involve a variety of win, place, and sometimes show betting, so we'll concentrate on both basic and advanced strategy in those sorts of events, assuming that there is an odds cap and, in most cases, the use of a scoreboard.

CHANGE YOUR WHOLE ATTITUDE

The first important thing to do, even before the outset of a contest, is to change your thinking and adjust your approach away from the way you typically play the races. Refocus on horse-playing within the confines of a tournament format, and remember that the name of the game is handicapping—not betting.

Since we're talking about a handicapping contest and not a betting contest, your usual money-making approach may not get you far in tournaments. Familiarize yourself with the intricacies of tournament play, and concentrate on the rules of the tournament you are about to enter. Prepare to attack the day's play with only one thing in mind: What is the best way to find the highest-priced winning horses in a limited time frame, and with a limited amount of straight bets at a specific number of tracks?

GATHER INFORMATION

Once your attitude has been adjusted toward tournament play, it's time to make sure you have all the necessary tools at your disposal. Arm yourself with as much information as you can, from *Daily Racing Form* to any other information you use, and do so before you walk in the front door of the contest venue.

Always do your work in advance, whether you prefer to handicap the night before or the morning of the contest. Bottom line: Don't just walk into a contest with a pencil and a track program and expect to be a contender.

Besides past performances, one of the most valuable pieces of information you can have is some historical data on the contest you are participating in. Whenever possible, try to find out what amount it has taken to win or qualify in previous years. Once you have that information at your fingertips, you will know what final amount of earnings you will need to shoot for and be able to adjust your playing strategy accordingly. Once you know how much you will likely need in order to win, you can set a goal for yourself and put a winning game plan in place that will be your guide throughout the duration of the contest.

Come prepared to track your own progress in the contest and constantly compare your position against not only your competition, but also your own goals. Wherever you might stand, be disciplined enough not to deviate from your predetermined plan of attack. Remember, even though you've handicapped the races in advance, you still want to save all your decision-making for the heat of battle, when it really counts.

AVOID DISTRACTIONS

Tournament play is meant to be fun, but it is also serious business that requires your full, undivided attention if you hope to be successful. That means you must do your homework and come to the contest ready to focus on the task at hand. Avoid all unnecessary distractions until after the contest is over.

MULTIPLE ENTRIES

Some contests allow you to play more than one entry, and this is always recommended when available, provided that paying for two entries is within your means financially. Two entries give you the ability to use your best plays on both tickets while leaving you the additional flexibility to spread your longshot plays out on multiple horses in races that are filled with overlays and primed for an upset. Essentially, this strategy gives you double the chance to connect with some of the boxcar-odds winners that everyone is always shooting for in tournaments.

Nothing is more frustrating in tournament play than singling out a race with vulnerable favorites, and proceeding to select the wrong 15-1 shot as you then watch a different longshot—one you had considered—roll home and pay $40. Buy two entries whenever you can, and chances are good that at least one of your two tickets' bankrolls will benefit from one or two extra longshots per contest.

PLAY YOUR RACES

Everyone excels at playing certain types of races more than others, and tournaments that offer betting on more than one track often give you the luxury of playing only the types of races that you prefer. For example, if you bet mainly turf races, you can probably find enough turf races on three or more race cards a day to allow you to play only those races in a particular contest. The same idea applies if you prefer maiden races or races with first-time starters, etc. Tournaments that offer multiple tracks give you enough of your preferred kinds of races that you can limit your play exclusively, or almost exclusively, to just the races you like to handicap.

NARROW DOWN THE CHOICES

In a contest with a limited number of tracks, or in contests where everyone must play all the same races, entrants won't have the luxury of picking and choosing their preferred spots. However, when full cards from three or more tracks are offered in a single contest, players should take advantage of the options and hone in mainly on the types of races they prefer. This is a prime example of narrowing your focus in order to gain a broader chance of winning.

Another way in which narrowing your focus can help your chances is in contests that use race cards from as many as five or six different racetracks. One such contest is the National Handicapping Championship, which uses as many as nine different tracks. Nine tracks means handicapping 80 to 90 races in order to keep up with all the action, and that can be a tall order for even the most dedicated horseplayer. If you try to handicap 80 to 90 races in a day, you probably won't do a very good job of it, because you won't be as thorough as you would be if you were handicapping a more manageable number of races, in the neighborhood of 40. When only 10 or 12 contest plays are called for in a day, handicapping more than 40 races may become counterproductive.

The best races to play in tournaments where you have a choice are the races with large, wide-open fields. It can be tough to find overlays and long prices in six-horse fields. Therefore, unless there is a specific horse you absolutely love in a short field, you may be better off limiting yourself to races with eight or more betting interests to increase your chances of finding an overlay.

Another good idea in multiple-track tournaments is to play only the three or four tracks or circuits that you are most familiar with. If you are a regular follower of New York, Southern California, and Chicago tracks, for example, it's probably unwise to suddenly start trying to become an expert on the ins and outs of racing at Lone Star Park just because it happens to be on the track menu of the contest you're currently playing. If you're traveling to a contest *at* Lone Star Park, it would certainly be to your advantage to learn as much as possible about that particular track. Otherwise, it will be advantageous for you to toss out the tracks you don't know much about in favor of paying more attention to the racing at the tracks you normally follow.

Taking it one step further, the tracks that are offered on the wagering menu at a contest should be one of the determining factors in the tournaments you choose to play. If a host track uses primarily its own races in its contest, and you don't know much about the host track's product, you just might be spotting too much home-track advantage to those with local knowledge for you to have a serious chance to win.

HANDICAP EARLY, DECIDE LATE

You don't show up at the track on the day of the races without handicapping the card in advance, and you definitely shouldn't show up at a contest without first taking a look at all the races you would consider playing once the contest begins. However, you would probably be better off handicapping contenders instead of locking yourself into hard-and-fast selections when it comes to tournament play. Once you've handicapped the contenders in the bettable races from the tracks you're comfortable playing, you can simply sit back and let the day's races unfold while waiting patiently for your contenders to go off at acceptable odds.

WHAT ARE ACCEPTABLE ODDS?

Talk to any of the best tournament players out there, and they'll universally tell you the same thing. You can't win contests by betting favorites. This is especially true in larger contests with a lot of entries, contests offering a small number of available races, and in contests that use a scoreboard.

Tournaments that use a scoreboard are essentially posting a target score for all to see, so basically anyone who can do math knows how much money he or she will need to take the lead or move into qualifying position. Players who fall far behind will obviously need to hit longshots in order to match the players out in front, who presumably have already done so.

Coming from behind can be difficult because the more entries there are in a contest, the more likely it is that other people are looking at the same longshots you're considering. This is especially true in contests that use just one or two tracks, or in contests where every entrant must play the same 10, 12, or 15 races. When there are a limited amount of races to choose from and a limited amount of horses in a race, several players are bound to select any given winner regardless of the price.

For example, if a mandatory race with 10 horses is included in a contest with 100 entries, the players' 100 selections are likely to be spread evenly among all 10 horses in the race because parimutuel rules do not apply in tournaments. In tournament play, there are likely to be as many plays on a 20-1 horse as there are on a 2-1 horse. When you think about it, this makes a lot of sense because you can let a bunch of 2-1 shots get past you in a contest, but the 10-1 to 20-1 shots you miss are the ones that kill you.

Generally speaking, you can't win tournaments by betting horses in the odds range below 5-1. In a hypothetical 10-race, win-betting-only contest, a highly unlikely perfect 10-for-10 day with a succession of 2-1 shots would net you only a $60 total ($6 x 10). An easier and more realistic way to reach and surpass a $60 total would be a three-win day with winners playing 15-1 ($32), 10-1 ($22), and 5-1 ($12). Most of us consider a three-win, seven-loss day (30 percent) well within our reach. The example above would be good enough for a $66 bankroll, which would be $6 ahead of the chalk player who went 10 for 10.

The point is, you don't need to bat 1.000 to win a tournament. It's possible to win with something like only 30 percent winners as long as those winners pay good prices.

Most tournament players understand that you won't win many contests betting favorites, but few can come up with the right combination of winning longshots and mid-priced horses needed to equal victory. The fact remains that the perfect game plan alone isn't enough to win a contest. You still need good handicapping.

Remember, a mix of good handicapping and a good strategy can often result in tournament victory, but good handicapping mixed with the wrong strategy probably won't be enough to get the job done.

Depending on how much you like a particular horse, your best bet is to plug away with contenders and live overlays in the 5-1 to 20-1 odds range. In contests where your handicapping is above average or better, you should be in contention to the end.

SEPARATE YOURSELF FROM THE MASSES

In contests with a lot of entries, upward of 200 to 300, the notion of separating yourself from the pack becomes more and more important. Accomplishing this in a large field can be difficult with anything short of one of your very best handicapping days when everything you touch turns to gold. Under normal circumstances in a large field, even a 10-1 winner or perhaps even two 10-1 winners are often not enough to separate yourself from the competition because so many of your rivals are bound to have made plays on the same horses you did.

The key to finding price horses in tournaments, whether they are below, at, or above the odds cap, is not to stab blindly at longshots.

Instead, try to find logical horses that are overlaid in the odds and/or get lost in the shuffle in large, evenly matched, questionable fields.

To gain an edge, use any information at your disposal that may not be common knowledge among your competition, such as breeding data in maiden and/or turf races. Many times you can unearth these types of longshots by handicapping races instead of handicapping horses, and picking the ones with vulnerable favorites. Once you've handicapped the right sort of race, handicap the contenders and then wait to see if you can find one that is being sent off at acceptable odds. Once you have all the pieces in place, fire away and hope you can hit the bull's-eye.

You'll know when you've handicapped the right sort of races to play because they'll be the ones producing all the high-priced winners. The leftover races will be the six-horse fields, and the races where the favorites keep winning. If one of these races is among the mandatory events, try to select the most likely winner and pick up whatever bankroll boost you can. If a race with a short field or a good favorite is not mandatory, go ahead and sit that race out and cheer home the favorites who you know can do you little harm.

CAP HORSES

Often, you won't be able to emerge from the masses without hitting that magical winner known to all tournament players as a cap horse. A winning horse that pays at or above a contest's odds cap is, of course, known as a cap horse and is the closest thing to the Holy Grail for tournament players. Cap horses are hard to come by, but they remain the best way to separate yourself from the pack and become an instant contender (and often an instant prize winner) in any contest you play in.

It pays to seek out at least a couple of these cap horses per day in a contest and swing for the fences. If you swing and miss, remember there's no difference for your bankroll between whiffing on a 2-1 shot or a 20-1 shot. You might as well go for it, because when you connect on a $42 cap horse, it is the equivalent of hitting seven 2-1 ($6) horses. (This is another example of why you can't win by betting favorites).

In a handicapping tournament, you always know when a cap horse has won because at least a dozen players are guaranteed to be standing up and screaming at the top of their lungs in jubilation. If 12 entrants in a 200-player contest hit a cap horse, that means that the other 188 players have $42 worth of catching up to do based only on win betting.

Most contests on the road to the National Handicapping Championship have a win-place format as opposed to just win betting. Under a $2-to-win and $2-to-place format, a cap horse is more likely to add something like $64 to a bankroll all in one shot ($42 to win + $22 to place based on a 20-1, 10-1 cap). Sixty-four dollars is an awfully big bomb to drop on your competition, and is certainly worth swinging for in a few select instances on each day of any contest you're playing. You're not always going to hit when you're aiming for 20-1 shots, but you are at least giving yourself a chance to win just by trying.

You're guaranteed to move into contention anytime you can pull a cap horse out of your hat. And even when your cap horse doesn't win, you can often still get a sizable boost to your bankroll if the horse in question can simply hit the board, finishing second in a win-place contest or third in an across-the-board format.

Occasionally, even a hit on a cap horse can be unsatisfying when your excitement is tempered by the realization that 10 or 12 of your tournament rivals just hit the same horse you did. That's when you realize that hitting a cap horse is not the end of the work you have to do to win, but only the beginning.

Since the theme here is the importance of separating oneself from the pack, we must raise the question, "Is it worth it to play a horse at odds above the odds cap?"

The cons of playing horses above the odds cap are obvious. Why play a 30-1 ($62) horse only to collect a maximum of $42 in the typical contest with a 20-1 cap? This is a valid question, and one that will always prevent a large percentage of would-be bettors from playing horses in this odds range. However, what better way to separate yourself from the pack than by sailing into waters that are often avoided by the majority of players?

Not receiving full track odds on horses above the odds cap can be discouraging, but the positives can definitely outweigh the negatives when these horses offer perhaps the best opportunities for you to put some distance between yourself and the competition. Besides, if you can really make a legitimate case for a cap horse at, say, 20-1, the fact that he drifts up to 30-1 or even 40-1 or above should not dissuade you from making a play.

DIRTY-SHIRT PICKS

The best longshots are always the ones that nobody else is smart enough, crazy enough, or desperate enough to come up with. I refer to these as dirty-shirt picks in honor of the desperate souls with stained shirts prowling deep in the bowels of the grandstand who eventually end up betting their final fin on a 40-1 shot instead of saving it for the bus fare home.

These picks are so far out there that you would almost have to be declared legally insane even to consider them. We're not talking about trip horses or "horses to watch" that sharpies have been waiting to bet in their next starts, and we're not talking about the 20-1 longshots that some computer programs will pick out, either. Dirty-shirt picks are those horses that you can make a case for once in a blue moon based on some arcane, obscure angle that you've had success with in the past and then tucked away in the cobwebs for just such an occasion. If you have a longshot angle that has worked for you, don't hesitate to use it during a tournament. Cap horses are nice, but a dirty-shirt winner that nobody else has is the true mother lode for contest players everywhere.

In the DRF/NTRA NHC III, Herman Miller hit a $75 dirty-shirt pick on a horse aptly named Crazy Star to help him win the championship.

TIMING IS EVERYTHING

When the contest is on and you have a limited number of bets, or "bullets," at your disposal, one of the most important concerns among tournament players is not just how, but when, to use the limited amount of precious firepower you are allotted. This is not really an important matter in cases where no scoreboard is provided or in events where the entire field must play the same mandatory races. Since you either have no information as to where your opponents stand or no choice as to when to make your plays in these kinds of contests, the timing of your plays is of no consequence from a strategic standpoint. However, in the typical contest with a scoreboard and a variety of races to choose from, when you use your bullets and whether you've saved any for the end of the contest can make the difference between winning and losing.

Players who save a few of their bullets until the end of a tournament have an important tactical edge over the players who don't. It is important to use every tournament bullet wisely, whether it is your first play of the contest or your last. Strategically speaking, however, you have a greater chance of making an educated decision on the best way to use your ammunition if you've saved it for the finish.

Bullets used throughout the duration of the contest are used for the purpose of bankroll building. Bullets saved for the end of a contest can, and should, be used strategically for potentially critical tactical moves and positioning. This positioning can involve anything from large plays by those playing catch-up to intricate maneuvers by those jockeying for position on the leader board.

Why use a remaining bullet late in a contest on a 20-1 shot when a winning 2-1 shot is all that stands between you and victory? Why bet a 5-1 shot late in a contest when you need nothing short of 20-1 shots in order to reach your goal?

Most contests involve some sort of mandatory betting format such as $2 to win and $2 to place, or $100 across the board, etc. However, a few contests, like Autotote's Sports Haven and the Bradley Teletheater Handicapping Challenges, give you $200 in mythical money per play to spend any way you want on straight bets (in $50 increments). You could, for example, bet $100 to win, $50 to place, and $50 to show, or $50 to win, $0 to place, and $150 to show, etc.

Under normal circumstances you should always maximize your play and bet strictly to win all the time ($200 to win in this case). The exception to this way of thinking would come at the end of a contest where a player has wisely elected to save a bet or two until the end. If a few dollars are all you need to leapfrog a rival, then perhaps a $200 place bet, or even a $200 show bet, can make it happen.

SAVE SOME PLAYS FOR THE FINISH

Players with bets remaining late in a contest can use them several different ways, both offensively and defensively. This can result in an interesting game of cat and mouse between the contenders in question, with the outcome of a tournament potentially hanging in the balance.

If Player A and Player B both have one bet remaining for the final race of a contest (or in a race where they are paired up against each other, as in Gulfstream's Turf-Vivor contest), and Player A has an $8 lead based on $2-to-win and $2-to-place wagers, Player B might shoot for a 9-5 or 2-1 favorite to make up the $8 deficit. Player A would then be forced to protect his lead with a bet on the same big favorite. Player B, anticipating Player

A's countermeasures, could instead switch his play to another, slightly higher odds horse in the race that would give him enough money to pass Player A. Player A has the lead, but in a way, Player B holds the upper hand in this instance because Player B can play offensively while Player A must play defensively in order to protect his slim lead.

The point here is that this maneuvering could not take place at the end of a contest if either Player A or Player B had not saved a bullet for the finish. Without a remaining bet, a trailing player could not pass a leading player, and a leading player would be a sitting duck for any player or players who had conserved a bet for the finish.

The moral of the story is always to save at least one bet for the end of a contest because you never know if, or how, you're going to need it.

MAKE ADJUSTMENTS AND PLAY TO WIN

Whether or not you can manage to save some of your bullets for the end of a contest, it's still important to be able to adjust your play as a tournament progresses. If you get off to a good start, you may find that cap horses and dirty-shirt picks are not necessary for you to reach your monetary goal and win a contest. On the other hand, if you've gotten off to a slow start, you may need to forsake some 5-1 to 10-1 shots you might have otherwise considered in favor of some 15-1 to 20-1 shots you now need to get back into a contest.

Remember, if you finish out of the money in a contest, it doesn't matter whether you've lost by $2 or $2,000. You've still lost, and that's the bottom line. In the end, a loser with a respectable final dollar total may appear to have played better than a loser with a big, fat $0, but chances are that the player with $0 at least gave himself a chance to win by swinging for the fences and missing. When you see someone finish a contest with $0, you can be relatively sure he played the right strategy, but today just wasn't his day.

THE MENTAL GAME

In addition to being tests of handicapping skill and strategy, tournaments can also be tests of mental toughness. With an infinite number of opportunities to second-guess yourself during even a one-day handicapping tournament, the players who are able to stay focused and win the mental game are often also the ones with the best chance to win the overall contest.

20 STEPS TO TOURNAMENT SUCCESS

1) Adopt a tournament attitude
2) Familiarize yourself with the rules
3) Arm yourself with information
4) Estimate how much you'll need to win
5) Set a goal and form a game plan
6) Handicap early, but decide late
7) Avoid unnecessary distractions
8) Play more than one entry (when allowed)
9) Limit play to the tracks and races you prefer
10) Play mainly wide-open races with large fields
11) Handicap contenders in bettable races
12) Bet to win and don't bet favorites
13) Seek out horses at acceptable odds (5-1 and higher)
14) Don't stab blindly
15) Use cap horses to separate yourself from the pack
16) Watch the scoreboard closely
17) Use your bullets wisely
18) Adjust late in the contest
19) Save some ammo for the end
20) Refuse to choke or get down on yourself

Everyone should be allowed a mistake in a tournament, and many times an experienced player can rebound from an error and still go on to be successful. However, the frustration of a long losing streak or a costly miscue such as changing your mind and getting on a losing horse—or, even worse, getting off a winning horse—can be compounded many-fold if you let those mistakes get under your skin.

Play with confidence, but make sure not to get overconfident. Tournaments can humble even the cockiest of horseplayers, so avoid overconfidence, stay focused, and stick to your game plan to avoid choke jobs when the going gets tough.

When you're losing, don't get down on yourself. Instead, keep plugging away by making the best contest plays you can make at all times. Give the tide every chance to change before throwing up your arms and giving up.

Competition in tournaments is fierce, and there is a tiny margin for error when big prizes are up for grabs among large fields of talented handicappers. You may be able to get away with one mistake, but anything more than that and your hopes of winning are out the window.

A NOTE ABOUT PARTNERS

Many people opt to enter contests with a partner, particularly in events with very high entry fees or in tournaments that involve an excessive amount of races to handicap from several different tracks. Many contests allow partners, but in most cases the official entry may be only in one person's name. Additionally, in DRF/NTRA National Handicapping Championship qualifiers, keep in mind that only one person's name can go on an entry and only one person's name can go into the books as an official national-finals qualifier.

Aside from all the logistical matters, partnering up with another player can be a very productive strategy, and a way to cut entry-fee expenses in half. Several winners of the lucrative Championship at the Orleans have been partnerships, and it's no wonder partners do well in that contest and others like it, with a selection of nearly 100 races a day for three days from something like eight different tracks.

If you decide that partnering up with another player is for you, try to pick someone whose style of play complements your own, and someone whose strategy and philosophy on tournament play is the same as yours. Also, devise a method for dividing the chores equally in terms of both the workload and the number of decisions each player has to make.

Finally, make sure your partner is someone you can agree with and trust, and that you can get along with that person win or lose. Don't let silly squabbles and disagreements come between you, either during the contest or after it is over.

WE ARE THE CHAMPIONS, MY FRIEND

I approached 11 of the most prominent tournament players in the country and asked them to divulge their personal strategies and philosophies for playing and winning handicapping contests. These normally tight-lipped professionals, who have accounted for more than 30 handicapping-contest titles over the past two decades, agreed to give their own tips and advice on how to become a winning tournament player.

While each player is different, you will notice certain common themes among them, including the concepts of setting a goal, forming a game plan, playing longshots, being aggressive, and staying mentally tough.

Robert Bertolucci, *winner of the 1998 and 2000 Flamingo Reno Summer Challenges and the 2000 MGM Grand tour (a DRF/NTRA qualifier).*

I have been playing horses ever since I could walk. I live in Northern California and, like everybody else, had a constant dose of Russell Baze and Jerry Hollendorfer, which wasn't to my liking. Then I met a fellow horseplayer who introduced me into a new wave in horseplaying—handicapping tournaments.

The first strategy to have is to buy two or more entries. The reason is that you would like some extra plays for some longshots, and/or a backup entry if your first entry goes into the tank. Then I think you should set a goal on what point total you think will win the tournament and try to get to your goal. I play horses in the range of 6-1 to about 25-1. If a 50-1 shot wins I grin and bear it.

Besides good handicapping, the biggest thing you need to do is keep your cool no matter what happens. I used to get influenced by other players yelling when a longshot won who I didn't have. But if you blow your stack during a tournament, you also blow your chance of winning.

Good luck and have fun because that's what playing tournaments is all about.

David Crupi, *director of race book operations at the Mohegan Sun casino in Connecticut, and winner of the $60,000 Bradley Teletheater Handicapping Challenge in 1999 (DRF/NTRA qualifier).*

Successful tournament play can be attributed to a combination of basic strategies mixed with pure racing luck. There is a wide variety of handicapping techniques that will improve your chances of formulating the winning game plan.

First, scan the tournament races to determine which races offer value. Look for full fields with more than eight runners, turf races, and races with weak favorites to bet against. If possible, skip races with short fields and pass on low-priced favorites.

Come in with a basic strategy and a contingency plan. Play the horses you like, and go to Plan B if you start falling too far behind. Be patient, however, as many tournaments are won on the final day. Always stay upbeat, and don't be too hard on yourself for missed opportunities. When you move into contention, raise your focus to a higher level, dig deep, lock in, and stay the course.

Put into racing terms, the greatest of game plans can be toppled by bad running lines like "dwelt," "stumbled at the start," "checked," "lost rider," "eased in the stretch." However, by preparing in advance, you'll give yourself the best chance to win. The only true guarantee is that the player who throws in the towel is the player who will lose.

Ken Daniels, *co-host of the* Thoroughbred Hotline *radio show in Southern California, and winner of the August 2002 Suncoast Invitational and the 1991 World Cup of Thoroughbred Handicapping (Caesars Palace) tournaments.*

A contestant's mentality is the key to success in handicapping contests, and I believe there are three basic components that make up this winning mentality. No ego, no fear, and no hesitation.

First and foremost, dismiss your ego when playing tournaments. You cannot be concerned with saving face or worrying about what other people think. From experience, I have seen this concern virtually negate people's chances. A big ego is going to prevent you from winning, so leave it at the door.

Next, the no-fear factor is essential concerning the horse selections you make. In real-life betting, this fear factor prevents people from selecting certain priced horses. There should be no reason with your mythical bankroll not to choose a horse regardless of its price, as long as you truly believe your handicapping is valid.

Finally, no hesitation. I believe the wait-and-see attitude is the nature of how most people approach tournaments. Experience has taught me that hesitating and failing to take command from the start will hurt you rather than help you. Don't let opportunities pass you by.

Walk into a tournament with no ego, no fear, and no hesitation, and eventually you will have success if your technical handicapping skills are sufficient.

J. Randy Gallo, *owner of the Bettor Racing OTB in Sioux Falls, South Dakota, and two-time National Handicapping Championship qualifier. Winner of the March 1999 Championship at the Orleans along with his brother, Ross Gallo.*

Here's a simple strategy that I use to give myself a chance to be competitive in handicapping contests.

First, I set a target score to shoot at. That score is usually determined by the tournament format. In a win-bet-only format, you want to multiply your bankroll by 2 1/2. For example, in a two-day tournament with a total of 20 races at $200 per bet, your starting bankroll is $4,000 x 2 1/2, which equals a target score of $10,000. In a $2-win-and-place tournament with 20 races, your starting bankroll is $80. Allowing for lower place prices in this format, you want to try to double your bankroll making your target score $160.

If you chart scores of past tournaments, your target winning score should be comparable to past winning totals of that particular contest.

To reach your target score, you should focus on horses between 15-1 to 20-1 who you believe figure in the race. Favorites should not be used unless your target score has been reached or if you are jockeying for position late in a tournament. If, beyond this, you are still intent on playing beatable favorites, I'd like to congratulate you on your 97th-place finish.

Ross Gallo, *two-time National Handicapping Championship qualifier and winner of the Championship at the Orleans and the Fair Grounds Handicapping Contest in 1999 along with his brother, J. Randy Gallo.*

I've been going to handicapping contests for about five years, and during that time their popularity has grown many-fold because they're a blast to play in. Strategy in these tournaments varies depending on the format. Still, the soundest and most proven way to play is to ferret out logical and playable longshots generally starting around 10-1 and going up past the odds cap (usually 20-1).

The problem now is that too many guys are playing the right way, which makes the contests these days difficult to win. Five years ago, I could look at scores after the first day and see that most of the field was playing the wrong way and had no chance to win. Now, more than half the field are legitimate contenders. To win now, you need to be special and string big winners together. If you end up telling stories in the elevator about all the bad beats you took, it's even money you are not going to win the contest.

I must say that I am a *Daily Racing Form* junkie. I read DRF every day and I don't believe there is a better way to handicap horses than poring over the minutiae of the past performances and then seeing what a horse can do on the track. At some tournaments you see more computers than *Daily Racing Form*s. It's almost like a convention at Silicon Valley. I know for a fact that some computer programs are very effective, but come on. How can you pick winners without a little newspaper ink all over your hands?

Joe Girardi, *associate editor of* American Turf Monthly *magazine. Former National Handicapping Championship qualifier, and winner of the 1999 Suffolk OTB Handicapping Challenge.*

Strategies for each contest are different depending on the format, so read and understand the rules so you can figure out how to best attack the contest. Always look at the format and adjust your strategy accordingly.

In contests with a selection of races to choose from, you can't look for the most obvious winners. You will need to select at least 50 percent winners if your mutuels average only $10 (4-1). You also can't just think you have to pick 30-1 shots. Horseplayers realize it's not an easy task to select 30-1 horses on a regular basis. Pick mid-priced horses, and pick winners. These winners will build your bankroll and allow you the upper hand at the end of a contest by allowing you to expand the horses you are able to select.

In contests where everyone plays the same races, look for winners instead of only looking for certain priced horses. If there is an 8-5 shot that looks unbeatable in this sort of contest, take him to prevent other players from gaining ground on you.

In any contest, it is important to know which races to eliminate from your consideration. If there is a race where a 3-5 shot looks like an obvious winner, the race is a throw-out because 3-5 horses can't help you in contests. On the flip side, a big field with no clear-cut favorite where you have an opinion is an optimum contest play.

Break each race down into contenders and pretenders. If you have three equally rated horses who you think can win, let the odds decide your play. Throw out the pretenders and then look at which contenders would best help your bankroll. Stay focused, and don't keep looking at the scoreboard early in the contest. It can only sway your decisions away from what you came there to do. When the contest is coming to a close, then check out the leader board and decide what plays are the best to make.

David Gutfreund, *a.k.a the Thoroughbred Maven. Winner of multiple handicapping contests dating as far back as the 1980's, including a World Cup of Thoroughbred Handicapping at Bally's, back-to-back wins in the Pick the Ponies Invitational, and the Sam's Town Ultimate Challenge in 1995. Also finished second and fourth at the Orleans in the fall of 1998, and qualified for the National Handicapping Championship III by finishing third at Turf Paradise in 2001.*

The idea for anyone entering a handicapping contest is to win, but many contestants never even give themselves a chance at victory. This self-elimination comes in two forms: 1) playing too many low-priced horses, and 2) mentally getting down on yourself and/or not preparing properly.

The mathematical part is logical. If you plan on beating between 50 and 500 other contestants in any given contest, you are going to need to have some price horses along the way. I suggest working toward a target score. My simple formula for contests with win bets only is to try to triple your original bankroll. For contests with win and place wagers, try to multiply your bankroll 2 1/2 times, and for contests with across-the-board wagers try to double your bankroll.

The mental part is much trickier and a lot more subjective. It seems that it is quite imperative to be in a good frame of mind. Sometimes it's hard to stay positive after losing a photo or passing on a winner you had considered playing. Nevertheless, you must stay positive and be decisive. Without question, the more decisive you are, the less likely you will be to get down on yourself.

As far as preparation goes, the most important thing to me is to engage in a routine that I am comfortable with that includes plenty of sleep in multi-day events. A rested mind is much more likely to be in a good decision-making mode. Also avoid having too many outside influences during a contest. Anything that takes away from your concentration can only hurt your cause.

Also, don't make the mistake of overhandicapping. If you're in a six-track contest and don't know much about three of those tracks, just ignore them unless something jumps off the page at you.

Lastly, the prize structure in contests is almost always top-heavy, so therefore it makes sense to go for it and play to win!

Joe Hinson, *considered by many to be the king of the tournament circuit. Winner of eight tournaments between 1988 and 2000 including the National Handicapping Challenge at the Orleans in March 2000 and back-to-back wins at the Cal-Neva in 1988 and '89.*

The first thing I do in any handicapping tournament is come up with an initial goal which, if attained, will give me more than a 50 percent chance of winning. You can get previous information on what it has taken to win a particular contest from other entrants or the organizers of the event. You're not guaranteed of winning even if you hit your goal, but in most cases it should be good enough to finish in the top four.

To achieve a goal and have a reasonable chance of winning, you must be willing to play longshots of 8-1 or higher. It is extremely difficult to win any contest playing low-odds horses. For example, let's assume you have two bets left in a contest and need 18 more dollars to reach your goal. When you can play two horses at 8-1 odds or two horses at 7-2 in the final two races, you should always plan on playing the two horses at 8-1. Your chance of hitting at least one of these horses is approximately 18 percent (assuming a 15-percent takeout). If you try to make the same $18 with two 7-2 shots, the probability of doing so is only 3.6 percent! In this example, going for the higher-priced horses gives you almost five times the chance of reaching your goal.

I know that it sometimes can be difficult to play against low-priced horses you think will win, but those are not the kind of horses you need to bet in a handicapping contest.

Mike Labriola, *winner of six tournaments and more than $250,000 since 1984. Two-time National Handicapping Championship qualifier.*

For me to win a tournament, four things must happen. First, the scores must be relatively low. It's easier to be successful in events where the leader board doesn't sneak away from you. Second, you must handicap well. This rule applies to all except those who can win by picking names or while drinking heavily. Rule Three is to make no mistakes. Some of the common errors include tentativeness and disorganization. These are the things that can kill you, but they are inevitable over the course of time. If you can't eliminate them entirely, you must at least try to minimize them. Fourth and most important is to be lucky.

My advice to people who want to win tournaments starts with the recommendation that they play in as many of them as possible. There is a steep learning curve which must be conquered before you can seriously compete. Once a player reaches the comfort zone of belonging, they can attack the next goal of actually winning an event. Another good idea is to identify the profile of the races that are more easily discernible for you personally.

I think that while big odds are a needed part of the winning formula, they are not the sole ingredient. Almost all of my victories have included a generous sprinkling of mid-range winners that provided a perfect complement to the big bomb that gave me a running start.

Ralph Siraco, *host of* Race Day Las Vegas, Daily Racing Form *contributing writer, and turf editor of the* Las Vegas Sun. *Winner of the National Handicapping Challenge at the Orleans in 1998.*

It is important to realize that anyone can win a contest, and equally important to realize your chances for success increase with a game plan and consistency. Each tournament has different parameters that you must consider when mapping out a game plan for success.

My game plan starts with having several selections picked out before I enter the tournament area. After putting in my first, pre-selected picks, I settle down in my spot, get all of the pertinent late information, and have something to eat. That may sound simple, but if you don't get settled in you'll be playing catch-up at crucial points during the day when you need time to make decisions.

Next, I always play to a number that previous winners achieved in a tournament. This allows me to gauge how much I may need in order to win a competition. If a tournament is won by an average of 10,000 points, then that is the number I play to. I do not play to whoever the leader is on a particular day. I play to the final number I'll need for the tournament. The final points are what counts. Stay as consistent as you can, but be flexible enough to adjust if necessary to get to the number you'll need.

It is also important to remember that tournament play is different than playing the races with cash. Don't play the way you play in the real world of betting. Instead, make your tournament selections based on the rules of the contest. Tournaments and the real world of betting are not always the same, so know that difference.

Also remember that the final outcome relies on some degree of luck. That luck comes in three distinct categories: 1) the choices you make for your selections, 2) the racing luck you get from your picks, and 3) the luck of your competitors. If you are a sports fan or player, you know the meaning of streaks both good and bad, and know that you will need a break here or there to win.

Most importantly, have fun, and make sure you enjoy yourself, the tournament, and those you are playing against.

Steve Terelak, *third-place finisher in DRF/NTRA National Handicapping Championship I in January 2000. Multiple tournament winner, including the Flamingo Reno Winter Challenge in 1999 and the Turf Paradise Spring and Belmont Summer Challenges in 2000.*

Tournaments have a special quality about them, because they're a true test of one's handicapping skills conducted in a closed competitive setting. Overall, I'd say playing in them has made me a better handicapper.

Although the degree of difficulty is high, most events I've attended have been fun and rewarding. If you haven't played in a tournament, you've missed out on what I consider to be one of the more exciting and enjoyable forms of competition. It's kind of like playing chess and craps at the same time. It is truly a great feeling to be battling with your fellow competitors in a structured competition. So many of the same faces appear at these different events, and I think most of us understand why. It's gratifying to compete against friends and acquaintances who share the same passion.

The beauty of this game, especially tournaments, is that no one has the magic formula for winning, or more specifically, for winning all the time. There's always more than one way to skin a cat. Each event is structured differently. One of the first steps toward becoming a winning tournament player is to understand the rules of each event and tailor a game plan that best fits the parameters of the respective contest. Although luck does play a great role in the outcomes, elements such as discipline, patience, and skill are all key in order to compete at the top level.

Looking back, I'd have to say that I learned something from every one of my losses. I've adopted a more flexible style. In my opinion, too rigid a style takes some of the spontaneity out of handicapping and ultimately diminishes one's personal enjoyment of a tournament. Although still disciplined in my approach, I continue to experiment with alternative forms of mental preparation, styles of play, and sources of information. I've also incorporated things into my own style from the people I've met at tournaments, who happen to be some of the sharpest players I've ever met.

I learned early on how difficult it was to win, and when I finally did win it was a great feeling in many ways. Other times I thought I played well enough to win only to find that others were better on that day. I marvel at how good players are at their home tracks. Having traveled to contests at other racetracks across the country, it can be a humbling experience to go up against the locals. I'm no longer surprised by some of the great scores these folks post.

As for advice, I will say this. The mental side is just as important as the mechanical skills a tournament player may possess. Keep an open mind, pay attention, trust your instincts, be aggressive, and don't give up. Finally, play to win, but don't take it all too seriously. Ultimately, it's still just a game.

5

THE DAILY RACING FORM/NTRA NATIONAL HANDICAPPING CHAMPIONSHIP

MANY OF THE biggest handicapping contests held over the last 20 years have been won by a handful of top tournament professionals. To date, however, none of those tournament pros has won the Daily Racing Form/NTRA National Handicapping Championship.

The first three editions of the National Handicapping Championship have belonged exclusively to the common, everyday horseplayer, as Steven Walker (2000), Judy Wagner (2001), and Herman Miller (2002) proved when they took on the professionals and beat them at their own game to take home $100,000 and the title of DRF/NTRA Handicapper of the Year. Walker, Wagner, and Miller were not known to regulars on the tournament trail before their national-championship victories, but each is now a household name among horseplayers everywhere who are seeking the title of Handicapper of the Year.

The DRF/NTRA National Handicapping Championship was created in 1999, and in the short period of time since then it has already become the premier horse handicapping tournament in existence. Period.

The national championship offers a purse of $212,000, and while a couple other contests might offer more prize money, none can come close to matching the prestige of this annual two-day event in Las Vegas.

There are several reasons for the allure of the National Handicapping Championship, beginning with the fact that it is an invitation-only event. You can't buy your way into this tournament. The only way to play is to earn your way into the national finals by qualifying in a recognized regional qualifying tournament. These preliminary events serve as a proving ground for would-be finalists who must first test their mettle against hungry handicappers like themselves. Many qualifying contests are world-class tournaments in their own right, and many of the qualifiers from these events are already major prize winners before they even reach the National Handicapping Championship. Most qualifiers have earned cash prizes, some amounting to tens of thousands of dollars, and all have earned free trips to Las Vegas including airfare and hotel accommodations at the host property and free entries into the National Handicapping Championship field.

Handicappers can play in as many qualifying contests as they wish, but can qualify only once per year, ensuring that all finalists begin the national tournament on equal footing. No qualifier ever pays an entry fee to play in the National Handicapping Championship. Once you qualify, you are guaranteed a free shot at the grand prize of $100,000, plus a share of additional team prizes, daily prizes, and bonus money.

A lot of tournaments offer a lot of prize money, but in the National Handicapping Championship, prize money is only the start of the total prize package. One of the unique things about this tournament is the fact that the winner receives his or her trophy at the Eclipse Awards dinner, which is held annually to honor the top horses, owners, breeders, trainers, jockeys—and now horseplayers—in the sport of Thoroughbred racing.

The grand prize for the DRF/NTRA National Handicapping Championship includes:
- **Prize money of $100,000**
- **Paid trip to the Eclipse Awards for trophy presentation**
- **Free chance to defend title in next year's NHC finals**
- **Name recognition in DRF and other national media**

HOW IT ALL GOT STARTED

The first qualifying events for the National Handicapping Championship were held in mid-1999, and the first DRF/NTRA national final was held in January 2000 in the race and sports book of the MGM Grand in Las Vegas. *Daily Racing Form* chairman and publisher Steven Crist came up with the idea for the National Handicapping Championship in 1998.

"This whole contest evolved from a casual conversation I had with [commissioner] Tim Smith of the NTRA," said Crist. "He asked me for suggestions on the Eclipse Awards dinner and I said, 'How about honoring an actual horseplayer?' To me, that's the greatest thing about this contest. Whoever wins it is going to get a trophy at the Eclipse Awards, and the industry will be saying something it needs to say more often: 'You, the fan, are as important to this business as the owner, the breeder, the trainer, and the jockey.'"

The idea for the championship quickly gained momentum within *Daily Racing Form* and the NTRA, with officials from both groups meeting often throughout early 1999 to hammer out the rules and procedures, create a format, and line up qualifying sites.

The first thing that was decided was that qualifying players would never have to pay to play in the national championship, and the only way to get into the championship was to qualify. The original purse was set at $200,000, but the contest still needed a way to come up with the substantial amount of purse money. Traditionally, handicapping tournaments get their purse money from players' entry fees, but that was not going to be an option in this case. With no money coming from the players, it was decided that the purse money would need to come from the tracks and OTB's that would host the preliminary events. The operators of these qualifying sites agreed, eager to participate in the promotion, and thus the National Handicapping Championship was born.

The original format for attaining the purse money is still in place. Participating NTRA-member tracks, OTB's, race books, and on-line venues play a flat membership fee, which allows them to host sanctioned qualifying contests. The tracks pay $1,000 for every qualifying player they send to the national finals, and also agree to pick up the tab for travel and hotel expenses for at least their top four finishers. The tracks pay the freight, and then *Daily Racing Form* and the NTRA take the ball from there on out to create, promote, market, and stage the national-finals event with the help of the host property in Las Vegas.

THE FIRST THREE CHAMPIONS

None of the first three winners of the National Handicapping Championship tournament had ever won a major tournament before qualifying for the national finals. The trio of winners represents a cross-section of horse-racing fans and handicappers from around the country.

The 2000 Handicapper of the Year, Steven Walker, was a 45-year-old state environmental worker from Lincoln, Nebraska. The 2001 winner, Judy Wagner, was a 50-year-old retired owner of a sports travel service. And the 2002 winner, Herman Miller, was a 50-year-old landscaper from Oakland, California. No professional handicappers in that bunch, just three average horseplayers who walked into the National Handicapping Championship as underdogs and walked out $100,000 richer.

PRIZE BREAKDOWN

The winners aren't the only ones making money at the National Handicapping Championship. The entire field has a free shot at playing for some serious money, and there are plenty of different prizes to go around. The total purse of the national finals is $212,000, which is divided up into $158,000 in individual prize money, $32,000 in team prize money, $12,000 in daily prize money ($6,000 per day), and $10,000 in bonus prize money ($5,000 per day).

The complete prize breakdown for the DRF/NTRA National Handicapping Championship is as follows.

Individual Prizes

1st	$100,000	4th	$5,000
2nd	$30,000	5th	$3,000
3rd	$10,000	6-10th	$2,000 each

Team Prizes

1st	$20,000 ($5,000 x 4)
2nd	$8,000 ($2,000 x 4)
3rd	$4,000 ($1,000 x 4)

Daily Prizes

1st	$3,000
2nd	$2,000
3rd	$1,000

Bonus Plays

$5,000 each day

FORMAT

The format for the National Handicapping Championship has remained basically the same throughout the early history of the event, and is designed to be the best possible test of overall handicapping ability. Players make 15 mythical $2 to win and $2 to place wagers on each day of the two-day contest. Eight of the wagers are on mandatory races that every player in the contest must bet. The remaining seven plays per day are optional bets that are left to the discretion of the players.

The contest takes betting on a selection of eight different tracks representing the entire country. Due to the timing of the national finals in January, the tracks traditionally selected to be part of the tournament are Aqueduct, Fair Grounds, Laurel, Golden Gate, Gulfstream, Santa Anita, Turf Paradise, and daytime races, if any, from either Sam Houston or Turfway.

The mandatory races are selected by a panel of handicappers including *Daily Racing Form* national handicapper Mike Watchmaker, tournament director Jeff Sotman, and a representative from the host property's race book.

Watchmaker said he and the panel look for "large, well-matched fields representing all of the tracks in the contest. The mandatory races will go from one end of the class spectrum to the other. We're trying to make it as difficult as possible."

Players in the National Handicapping Championship compete both as individuals and as members of four-person teams representing their qualifying sites. Scores are computed by adding the total combined mutuel payoffs of all winning selections, with an odds cap of 20-1 ($42) to win and 10-1 ($22) to place.

In the team portion of the competition, each foursome is not necessarily working together as a unit. Instead, team scores are simply arrived at by adding the individual scores of the four team-members.

As additional perks, daily prize money of $12,000 and bonus prize money of $10,000 are also up for grabs in the national championship. The idea is to put checks into the hands of as many different finalists as possible over the course of the two-day contest. Prizes go to the top three highest-scoring players on each day of the contest. Bonus prizes go to the contestants who correctly pick the most winners in a separate horse-vs.-horse proposition wager. In this prop bet, two horses of equal ability are chosen in each of the eight daily mandatory races. You just select which horse you think will beat the other, and you win or split the $5,000 daily prize if you get the most correct.

FIELD SIZE

The size of the field for the National Handicapping Championship varies from year to year, and is determined by the number of qualifying sites that participate. In the first three handicapping championships, the field has been as small as 160 players (40 qualifying sites) in NHC I, and as large as 204 players (51 qualifying sites) in NHC II.

In NHC III, the contest began offering an exemption to the previous year's defending champion, which allows the reigning DRF/NTRA Handicapper of the Year to return to the national finals even if he or she fails to requalify. This is a somewhat controversial exemption, but having the current champion in the contest does add an element of excitement to the event. Also, because the defending champion is not part of a four-person team (unless he requalifies), he is not eligible to compete for the $32,000 in team prize money offered in the contest.

NHC III in January 2002 drew a smaller field of 177 players (44 teams plus the defending champ) because some tracks temporarily dropped out of the NTRA in 2001. In the future, expect field sizes in the National Handicapping Championship to include at least 200 players with more and more tracks, race books, and organizations signing on every year.

ATMOSPHERE

Qualifying players can expect to encounter a lively atmosphere when they arrive at the National Handicapping Championship tournament. Players are welcomed at check-in and given a packet containing the rules and betting procedures. Qualifiers then can familiarize themselves with the tournament venue and are later assigned a seat in the contest area.

The National Handicapping Championship is more than just a contest. It's an entire three days of activities, beginning with a welcoming cocktail party on the night before the event, and ending with an awards banquet at the conclusion of the action, where final standings and prize winners are announced.

For horseplayers who are accustomed to betting their horses in private, the scene at the national championship will be a major change of pace. Several media members are always on hand to cover the tournament, from *Daily Racing Form* writers to reporters from local Las Vegas television, radio, and newspaper sources. The National Handicapping Championship has also received coverage from national magazines such as *Sports Illustrated, ESPN The Magazine,* and *Penthouse,* to name a few. In the past, TVG network has also provided live coverage.

The first three Daily Racing Form/NTRA National Handicapping Championship winners earned their crowns in different ways. Three winners, three stories. Here is how the National Handicapping Championship has been won.

Steven Walker, 2000: Walk This Way

Michael J. Martin/Horsephotos

The first DRF/NTRA Handicapper of the Year, Steven Walker, qualified for the national finals in a contest at Horsemen's Park in Omaha, Nebraska. Walker, 45, from Lincoln, Nebraska, picked six winners out of a nine-race card at Keeneland to beat 399 other players in the third of Horsemen's Park's four qualifying events in 1999 to earn his trip to Las Vegas.

Walker joined 159 other finalists from 40 different racetracks, OTB's and casinos in NHC I on January 7-8, 2000, at the MGM Grand in Las Vegas. The qualifiers hailed from 27 different states and Canada and ranged in age from 25 to 80 years old.

For two days, the MGM Grand race and sports book was transformed into the center of the horse-racing universe. Giant digital boards, usually reserved for football, basketball, hockey, and boxing lines, were turned into scoreboards displaying the names and scores of every finalist. TVG network had a booth set up at the back of the contest area to provide live television coverage of the inaugural event.

The format of the first contest was a real handicapping marathon consisting of 20 mythical $2 win and $2 place bets on each day of the two-day event. Ten plays per day were mandatory, and 10 were optional. Ten tracks were open for betting including Aqueduct, Fair Grounds,

Golden Gate, Gulfstream, Laurel, Penn National, Sam Houston, Santa Anita, Turf Paradise, and Turfway. This format, including a total of 40 race plays from 10 day and night tracks, proved to be so demanding that the contest was later scaled down to 30 plays from only day tracks in subsequent years.

Walker emerged from this grueling test with a total of $305.40 to win the contest over runner-up Maury Wolff from Alexandria, Virginia, who finished with $285.20.

Walker worked his way into 10th place at the end of the first day of the tournament, and then came up big on Day Two by hitting four of his first five bets. Walker hit the lead with a $40.40 winner (Star of Rio) at Gulfstream Park, and then cashed his last three bets including a $21.20 winner (Smilin' Forbes) at Sam Houston to cement the victory. In total, Walker hit eight winners out of a possible 20 on the second day of the contest to earn his crown.

"I did well both early and late," Walker said in reference to his success on Day Two. "After the good start, I lost seven bets in a row and then made most of my money the last hour and a half. I needed that win [Star of Rio at $40.40] to build my confidence back up, then I studied hard and relaxed to see what was happening in the standings."

Walker rebounded from a cold streak, relaxed and regrouped, and then hit a couple longshots to win the contest, demonstrating just how important the mental game is in tournament play. With a pair of heavyweights on his tail, Walker stayed the course and held on over both Wolff and multiple tournament winner Steve Terelak of Burbank, California, who finished third with $277.

Wolff finished the first day of the contest with only $25 but then made an enormous $260.20 move on the second day to finish second. Wolff hit several high-priced winners during his Day Two run. To put his rally in perspective, Wolff's second-day total alone would have been good enough for fifth place overall.

Terelak's third-place finish put the finishing touch on an incredible year of tournament play, which also included a win in the $153,600 Flamingo Reno Winter Challenge, a third in the $409,000 National Handicapping Challenge at the Orleans Casino, and a second in Turf Paradise's $34,200 qualifying event. Interestingly, one of Terelak's key winners in the national finals, Rosie's Colonel ($20.60), was the very same horse he hit at Turf Paradise in order to qualify a month earlier.

NATIONAL HANDICAPPING CHAMPIONSHIP I
JANUARY 7-8, 2000

INDIVIDUAL WINNERS

Place	Player	Representing	Bankroll*	Prize Money
1st	Steven Walker	Horsemen's Park	$305.40	$100,000
2nd	Maury Wolff	Bettor Racing OTB	$285.20	$30,000
3rd	Steve Terelak	Turf Paradise	$277.00	$10,000
4th	Brian MacClowry	Turf Paradise	$276.40	$5,000
5th	Rose Ann Yanik	Arlington	$255.20	$3,000
6th	Allen Schafer	Aqueduct	$242.20	$2,000
7th	Louis Noto	Philadelphia	$234.80	$2,000
8th	Bob Randazzo	Thistledown	$231.30	$2,000
9th	Mike Forbes	Del Mar	$229.00	$2,000
10th	William Landers	Foxwoods Casino	$228.00	$2,000

TEAM WINNERS

1st	Turf Paradise		$784.80	$20,000
	(Ken Hoskins, Rick Leoni, Brian MacClowry, Steve Terelak)			
2nd	Del Mar		$686.70	$8,000
	(Mike Forbes, R. Kelsey Johnson, Michelle McConnell, Patricia Timm)			
3rd	River Downs		$681.70	$4,000
	(Jim Conner, Lou Frank, Mike Hopewell, Chris Long)			

BONUS WINNERS

Day One	Alex Slivensky	Hoosier Park	$5,000
Day Two	David Morrone**	Foxwoods	$2,500
	Michael Markham**	Fairplex	$2,500

There were no daily prizes awarded in the first National Handicapping Championship.

* The format of NHC I consisted of 20 $2 win and $2 place wagers a day.

** David Morrone and Michael Markham tied and split the $5,000 Day Two bonus.

The first National Handicapping Championship was not without controversy. The announcement of the final order of finish was delayed slightly when it was discovered that unofficial second-place finisher Brian MacClowry of Phoenix had inadvertently placed one too many bets during the contest. His final play, a $17.40 winner, was deleted from his total, thereby moving him down to fourth place in the final standings.

MacClowry made up for the gaffe somewhat, however, by earning his share of the team title as a member of Team Turf Paradise. The foursome of Terelak, MacClowry, Ken Hoskins of Port Orchard, Washington, and Rick Leoni of Tucson split a $20,000 first prize for its victory over 39 other teams.

Alex Slivensky of Palatine, Illinois, was the story of the bonus competition. He earned $5,000 for going 9 for 9 in horse-to-horse matchup propositions.

Judy Wagner, 2001: Girl Power

Harold Roth/Horsephotos

Judy Wagner proved handicapping is not just a man's game when she became the first woman to capture the title of DRF/NTRA Handicapper of the Year by beating 203 other players in NHC II on January 12-13, 2001, at the MGM Grand in Las Vegas.

The 2001 National Handicapping Championship was the culmination of a year-long series of qualifying contests held at 51 racetracks, casinos, and OTB's, and even on horse-racing web sites. The 204 finalists ranged in age from 21 to 83, and hailed from 31 states, two Canadian provinces, and Milan, Italy.

The format in NHC II was basically the same as in NHC I, except that the contest was shortened slightly due to some complaints from players in NHC I that the 10-track, 20-race-per-day format was too demanding. The format of NHC II included $2 win and place wagering on 15 races per day (instead of 20) from eight different tracks (instead of 10). Players' bets were divided into eight mandatory plays per day (one from each track), and seven optional plays.

Wagner, who had qualified for the national finals on the strength of a third-place finish in the MGM Grand's $189,000 Grand Handicapping

Challenge held the previous May, claimed the home-field advantage at the MGM Grand helped her score the victory. "The MGM Grand has been good for me. I really believe I'm a horse for the course," Wagner joked.

Wagner, a retired director of a sports travel company, is a self-described racing fanatic. She travels to racetracks and tournaments around the country with her husband, Bryan Wagner, who is also an avid handicapper and National Handicapping Championship finals qualifier.

Bryan is a lifelong racing fan who introduced Judy to the sport and watched her rapid transformation into a serious player who lives, eats, and breathes Thoroughbred racing. Wagner had really only begun to learn the game five years before ascending to the title of DRF/NTRA Handicapper of the Year.

"Whoever thought someone like me, who has been handicapping for such a short time, could win a contest like this," Wagner said when she was awarded her first prize of $100,000. "I don't exactly fit the typical profile of a horseplayer."

Like NHC I winner Steven Walker, Wagner also got off to a strong start in the national finals and found herself in eighth place after the first day. She continued her assault on the leader board on Day Two and never fell out of the top 10.

Ironically, the horse that eventually won Wagner the championship ended up being a last-minute selection, which she was forced into making when her original intended play fell through in the closing minutes of the contest.

Wagner had saved her final "bullet" in the tournament for a longshot named Capo Di Capo, who was set to run against Tiznow in the day's feature race from Santa Anita, the Grade 3 San Fernando Breeders' Cup. Capo Di Capo was a late scratch, however, and Tiznow went on to turn in a winning performance.

With only one non-mandatory race remaining in the tournament, Wagner was forced to use her final contest wager in the Golden Gate Derby, which was scheduled to go off just minutes later. "I panicked because I've never bet a race from Golden Gate before in my life," she said.

Wagner's choice at Golden Gate was 15-1 longshot Hoovergetthekeys. "I liked the horse, but I had no idea he'd be the longest price on the board," Wagner said.

Hoovergetthekeys went on to win the race, and then survived a heart-stopping 10-minute jockey's objection to vault Wagner into the lead in the tournament. Hoovergetthekeys paid $33 to win and $12.20 to place, and the combined sum of $45.20 gave Wagner a winning total of

$237.70 for the two-day contest.

Her late good fortune was enough to edge runner-up Sean Nolan for the title by a mere $7.30. Nolan, a 35-year-old meteorologist and emergency management planner for the city of New York who had qualified for the finals at Delaware Park, settled for second prize of $30,000. The tournament's first-day leader, Gwyn Houston of Forest Hill, Maryland, finished third and earned $10,000 with a total bankroll of $225.40.

The previous year's champion, Steven Walker, who had qualified for a return trip to the National Handicapping Championship with a top finish in a contest at the Bettor Racing OTB in Sioux Falls, South Dakota, fell short of the leader board in 23rd place, but still managed to take home $3,000 in prize money. Walker blanked on the first day of the finals but then posted Saturday's highest daily total with a huge run that netted him $156.

The team competition went to the representatives of the Maryland Jockey Club tracks, Laurel and Pimlico. The four-person team of Maryland natives including Gywn Houston, Leo Feldman, Frank Okasaki Jr., and Bob Ordakowski shared the top team prize of $20,000.

The highlight of the bonus competition was on the second day of the contest when Craig Koff of Boca Raton, Florida, and Chuck Berger of El Paso, Texas, split $5,000 for going a perfect 8 for 8 in the day's horse-vs.-horse matchup proposition.

NATIONAL HANDICAPPING CHAMPIONSHIP II
JANUARY 12-13, 2001

INDIVIDUAL WINNERS

Place	Player	Representing	Bankroll	Prize Money
1st	Judy Wagner	MGM Grand	$237.70	$100,000
2nd	Sean Nolan	Delaware Park	$230.40	$30,000
3rd	Gwyn Houston	Maryland Jky. Club	$225.40	$10,000
4th	Terry Severson	Canterbury Park	$219.60	$5,000
5th	Mary Walker	Cal. State Fair	$211.40	$3,000
6th	Francis Moore	Sam Houston	$208.00	$2,000
7th	Robert Ferguson	Keeneland	$207.00	$2,000
8th	Harry Nelson	Fairplex	$200.80	$2,000
9th	Rich Laughlin	Big Fresno Fair	$200.60	$2,000
10th	Robert Cliff	MGM Surf & Turf	$195.60	$2,000

TEAM WINNERS

1st   Maryland Jockey Club $644.60 $20,000
        (Gwyn Houston, Leo Feldman, Frank Okasaki Jr., Bob Ordakowski)
2nd   Canterbury Park $545.20 $8,000
        (Ron Hafner, Dan Hastings, Noelle Severson, Terry Severson)
3rd   MGM Grand Surf & Turf $539.40 $4,000
        (Peter Brooks, Robert Cliff, Maury Joffe, Massimo Reynaud)

DAILY WINNERS – Day One

1st	Gwyn Houston	Maryland Jky. Club	$3,000
2nd	Robert Cliff	MGM Grand	$2,000
3rd	James Eaton	Prairie Meadows	$1,000

DAILY WINNERS – Day Two

1st	Steven Walker	Bettor Racing OTB	$3,000
2nd	Robert Ferguson	Keeneland	$2,000
3rd	Francis Moore	Sam Houston	$1,000

BONUS WINNERS

Day One   Masahide Nakagawa (Hol), Joel Johnson (HPO), Chris Burden
          (Cal. State Fair), Don Duff (CD), Bill Marquis (PrM), Robert
          Pinney (Haw), Tom Scolaro (Mohegan Sun), Marvin Still (CD) –
          $625 each
Day Two   Chuck Berger (Sun), Craig Koff (FG) – $2,500 each

Michael J. Martin/Horsephotos

Herman Miller, 2002: It's Miller Time

The race and sports book at the MGM Grand in Las Vegas hosted the annual Daily Racing Form/NTRA National Handicapping Championship for the third time on January 25-26, 2002. A field of 177 horseplayers including defending champion Judy Wagner attended the event to compete for a purse of $212,000, including a grand prize of $100,000.

The winner of the Championship was Herman Miller, a 50-year-old landscaper from Oakland, California, who had the distinction of being the final player to qualify for NHC III. Just weeks earlier, Miller was the fourth and final qualifier out of the final national qualifying contest held at Golden Gate Fields in late December 2001. It was the first handicapping contest Miller had ever played in.

Miller defeated 159 men and 17 women ranging in age from 21-year-old Randy R. Gallo from Jupiter, Florida, to 82-year-old Ruth Beaufait from Arcadia, California. The field was divided into 44 teams of players who had qualified at a total of 48 different sites in 65 different contests.

Miller hit nine winners in the 30-race national-finals tournament while on his way to a contest-winning bankroll of $205.30, based on $2 win and $2 place bets on 15 races per day. He alternated for the lead throughout both days of the contest. On Day One, Miller rocketed to the top of the standings thanks to his dirty-shirt pick on Crazy Star in Gulfstream Park's 10th race. Crazy Star paid $75.20 to win (capped at $42) and $22.60 to place (capped at $22), and Miller was the only player in the room who had it.

He entered the second day of competition in first place and then lost his lead for a while on Saturday as other players used early bets to reach the top of the standings. Miller stormed back, however, eventually putting together a three-race winning streak late in the contest to seal the victory.

Miller hit several long-priced horses on the first day of the event to reach the top of the leader board, but played sensible mid-priced horses on Day Two in order to stay on top. He began his late rally with Torgan ($11.20 to win, $6.80 to place) at Fair Grounds, continued his charge with Goldworks ($12 to win, $5.60 to place) at Turf Paradise, and put the icing on the cake with Alystone Lane ($11.20 to win, $6.80 to place) at Santa Anita.

The new champion was entering his 15th year as a dedicated horseplayer at the time of his National Handicapping Championship victory. He attributed his success throughout the tournament to going against bad favorites in wide-open races, and then went into further detail about the secrets of his success.

"If it's a full field and I think the favorite is going to lose, then I use my own system to find the winner," said Miller. "I take the raw data from the *Racing Form* and rely heavily on the Beyer Figures. Then I come up with my own formula in which I coordinate my speed/class/pace 'spectrum' and decide which is more important in that race. I also use other handicapping methods, with jockeys and trainers and the like."

Miller received $104,000 in prize money including the first-place check for $100,000, a $3,000 daily prize for posting Day One's top score, and $1,000 for being part of the third-place team representing Golden Gate Fields. He received his check at a post-contest awards din-

NATIONAL HANDICAPPING CHAMPIONSHIP III
JANUARY 25-26, 2002

INDIVIDUAL WINNERS

Place	Player	Representing	Bankroll	Prize Money
1st	Herman Miller	Golden Gate	$205.30	$100,000
2nd	Tim O'Leary	Maryland Jky. Club	$189.00	$30,000
3rd	Don Speaks	Turf Paradise	$183.00	$10,000
4th	Sid Weiner	MGM Grand	$179.30	$5,000
5th	John Martin	River Downs	$167.30	$3,000
6th	Frank Auriemma	Aqueduct	$165.20	$2,000
7th	David Brownfield	Hoosier Park	$164.60	$2,000
8th	Richard Nilsen	Keeneland	$161.90	$2,000
9th	Bobby Brendler	MGM Grand	$157.00	$2,000
10th	Jesus Bravo	Los Alamitos	$154.00	$2,000

TEAM WINNERS

1st	Keeneland "A"	$506.10	$20,000
	(Don "Hee Haw" Alvey, Tim Holland, Tony Martin, Richard Nilsen)		
2nd	Suffolk Downs	$478.10	$8,000
	(Kevin Blair, Richard Falvey, Charles Giovino, Robert Goral)		
3rd	Golden Gate	$473.00	$4,000
	(Wei Fang, Herman Miller, Tom Rufini, Carl Standley)		

DAILY WINNERS – Day One

1st	Herman Miller	Golden Gate	$3,000
2nd	Richard Nilsen	Keeneland "A"	$2,000
3rd	David Brownfield	Hoosier Park	$1,000

DAILY WINNERS – Day Two

1st	John Martin	River Downs	$3,000
2nd	Harry Ellam	Autotote-Sports Haven	$2,000
3rd	Brant Bowen	Fair Meadows	$1,000

BONUS WINNERS

Day One	Dominic Calise (Los Alamitos), Brian Deeley (Breeders' Cup), Walter Ohler (FG) – $1,666.66 each
Day Two	Wilfred Asprer (Cal. Fair), James Coffey (AP), Brian MacClowry (Sun) – $1,666.66 each

ner at the MGM Grand, and later accepted his DRF/NTRA Handicapper of the Year award at the Eclipse Award ceremonies in Miami Beach, Florida, early the next month.

Second-place in NHC III went to Tim O'Leary, a 45-year-old budget manager from Newville, Pennsylvania, who finished with a bankroll of $189 after spending almost the entire contest in the top five on the leader board. O'Leary earned $30,000, and finished just six dollars ahead of third-place finisher Don Speaks of Oceanside, California.

As always, $32,000 in prize money was offered in the separate team competition, which was won by the first of two four-member Keeneland teams to compete in NHC III. The foursome of Don "Hee Haw" Alvey from Louisville, Rich Nilsen and Tony Martin from Lexington, and Tim Holland from Midway, Kentucky, split the $20,000 team first prize.

WHAT'S NEXT?

Starting with National Handicapping Championship IV in January 2003, the contest will move from the MGM Grand to its new home at the Bally's race and sports book in Las Vegas. The new location accommodates more people than the MGM Grand and will give the event room to grow in the years ahead.

From the first three years of the national championship, we have learned that you don't need to be a professional handicapper in order to win the big tournaments. The winners have had very few things in common, except for the fact that they were all highly dedicated horseplayers who got themselves into contention early in the contest and then played the mental game perfectly and didn't crack under pressure.

With the proper strategy, the right amount of hard work, and the necessary mental toughness, you too can beat the pros and take home $100,000. Get yourself to your local qualifying contest, play hard, and earn your ticket to the National Handicapping Championship. You could be the next DRF/NTRA Handicapper of the Year.

6

DRF/NTRA QUALIFYING-CONTEST INDEX

IT IS NOT an exaggeration to say that a qualifying spot in the National Handicapping Championship is one of the most coveted and sought-after prizes for horse handicappers. A qualifying spot in the tournament is an invitation to the party of the year for horseplayers.

It is estimated that as many as 45,000 people per year play in at least one DRF/NTRA qualifying handicapping contest in an attempt to win prize money and earn their way to the National Handicapping Championship. Those 45,000 players are competing for just under 200 available qualifying spots in the national finals, which, in part, is what makes the event so special. Many players compete in more than one contest, with several even traveling from city to city in search of berth in the championship.

Some of the biggest horse bettors in the country have moved the National Handicapping Championship to the top of their list of priorities. One of America's biggest pick-six players, J. Randy Gallo of Jupiter, Florida, bets seven-figure dollar amounts annually and has been known to hit big carryovers everywhere from Saratoga to Santa Anita. Gallo qualified for the 2001 national championship in a handicapping contest at the Mohegan Sun casino in Connecticut on October 19, 2000, the same day he took down a $648,076 pick-six pool at Santa Anita.

Gallo's comment: "Believe it or not, I was more excited about qualifying for the contest."

Horseplayers obviously take the National Handicapping Championship seriously, but dedication alone isn't enough to get you to the national finals.

The road to the National Handicapping Championship always has and always will go through the qualifying contests, which are held annually at dozens of tracks, OTB's, casinos, and on-line venues throughout North America.

Following is an index of all current DRF/NTRA National Handicapping Championship qualifying contests. Many of these contests have very little in common, except for the fact that each is a gateway to the national finals in Las Vegas.

The information in the index is up-to-date through the qualifying contests of 2002, but all information is subject to change. With a few exceptions, contestants must be at least 21 years old in order to participate in DRF/NTRA qualifying contests. A few tracks allow players 18 and older to compete in their contests, but you absolutely must be 21 or older to qualify for the National Handicapping Championship.

Most contests include free admission, parking, programs and/or *Daily Racing Form*s and lunch, but space prohibits mentioning these details in the write-ups for each and every contest.

This index is intended to be a handy reference guide that you can use throughout the year as you plan your own schedule and strategy to qualify for the next DRF/NTRA finals. Use it over and over again to stay one step ahead of the pack on the road to the National Handicapping Championship.

The index contains valuable information on each contest including my tips on how to win. Every DRF/NTRA qualifying contest has been rated on a scale of 1 to 5 in terms of overall quality, value, and the ratio of entrants to qualifiers.

Overall ratings are based on a contest's quality, taking into account all factors including its rules, format, atmosphere, prize structure, value, prestige, and field size.

Value ratings are based on a contest's entry fee, and prize money, and whether the contest pays back all entry fees in the form of prize money or charges a takeout. Value ratings are not given for free contests.

The final rating is a qualifier rating, which is based on the ratio of entrants to national-championship qualifiers in any given DRF/NTRA contest.

The index contains a total of 44 contests, and tournament enthusiasts should try to play in as many of these events as possible throughout the year. For those who plan special trips to contests around the country, I have given my highest recommendation to 16 contests based the ratings outlined above. These are the contests throughout the year that, in my opinion, should not be missed.

INDEX TO QUALIFYING CONTESTS

ARLINGTON PARK HANDICAPPING CONTEST   *Recommended

Where: Arlington Park, Arlington Heights, Illinois (Chicago area)
When: September
Who: Limited to 150 entries
How much: Entry fee is $125. Twin Spires Club Members pay $100.
Purse: $15,000
Scoreboard? Yes, updates follow each mandatory race
DRF/NTRA qualifying SPOTS: 4

Contest Rating: 5
Value Rating: 3
Qualifier Rating: 4 (Ratio – 37:1)

■

Arlington hosts a one-day event in September to determine its four qualifiers to the DRF/NTRA National Handicapping Championship. The contest is limited to just 150 entries and costs $125 to enter. Twin Spires Club members get a discount and pay only $100. The entry fee includes admission to the track, *Daily Racing Forms,* programs, $10 in food and beverage tickets, and admission to the Starting Gate Theater, where the contest is held. The purse is $15,000, with $10,000 going to the winner, $3,000 for second, $1,500 for third, and $500 for fourth.

The Arlington Park contest consists of win and place wagering on 12 races including six mandatory Arlington races and six optional races from a selection of four assigned simulcast tracks. Each contestant will have a starting bankroll of $120, which will be divided into 12 different $10 win or place wagers. Contestants have the option of playing the entire $10 to win or to place, or may elect to divide their $10 bet between both win and place (example: $5 to win, $5 to place) as long as the total bet per race is no less or no more than $10. Win prices are capped at 20-1 ($42) and place prices are capped at 10-1 ($22). The top four finishers based on the total combined mutuel prices of their winning wagers will split the $15,000 prize fund and qualify for the National Handicapping Championship.

Why attend? Excellent contest atmosphere and format makes for an exciting event that is also a fair test of handicapping skill. The setup of this contest favors the players, with the field size limited to just 150 people, and an entry fee of only $125 or $100.

Why not? If you're not a Twin Spires Club member, you have to pay a $25 premium to enter the contest. The prize structure does not put the $25 premium back into the prize fund, so you are basically tossing that $25 out the window in order to compete. Conceivably, this contest could have a takeout as high as 20 percent if all 150 entrants were not Twin Spires Club members. Even so, incentives including admission ($5), DRF ($5), and a food and beverage allowance of $10 should offset most of the $25.

How to win: First and foremost, play your entire $10 per race to win in each and every contest wager with the possible exception of strategic plays late in the day. Since six Arlington plays are mandatory, make sure you pick the best six races on the card in terms of field size and value offered. You'll have plenty of races to choose from for your remaining six bets, so make sure you choose wisely while keying on your strongest opinions at the highest possible odds.

Where to stay: By far the best place to stay when visiting Arlington is the **Sheraton Chicago Northwest** (847-394-2000), located right next to the track on Euclid Ave. The hotel offers courtesy-van service to the track's front door. If you can't get a room at the Sheraton, try the **Hyatt Regency Woodfield** (847-605-1234) just five minutes from the track. The Hyatt is home to Knuckles Sports Bar, where you can show your loyalty to one Chicago baseball team or the other by choosing between the Slammin' Sammy Sandwich and the Big Hurt Roast Beef Sandwich.

Where to eat: Located a furlong outside the stable gate, **Jimmy D's** (1718 W. Northwest Hwy.; 847-255-1340) is a popular spot for both horsemen and horseplayers. There's a limited menu but enough cold brews at the bar to keep fans coming back for more. If you just can't get enough racing action, **Arlington Trackside OTB** (2200 W.

Euclid Ave.; 847-259-8400), located across Arlington's parking lot, offers a full menu catering to the night racing crowd. Intrepid travelers in search of finer fare can hit the road and head to **Bob Chinn's Crabhouse** in Wheeling (393 S. Milwaukee Ave.; 847-520-3633), or **Maggiano's** (1901 E. Woodfield Rd.; 847-240-5600) in Schaumburg for Italian fare including killer rigatoni in vodka sauce and the biggest meatballs you've ever seen. Be prepared for long waits.

Contact info: For more information, call (847) 385-7765.

AQUEDUCT HANDICAPPING CHALLENGE   *Recommended

Where: Aqueduct Race Course, Jamaica, New York
When: November
Who: Limited to 200 entries (up to two entries per person)
How much: $300 entry fee
Purse: $60,000
Scoreboard? Yes, every bet for every player
DRF/NTRA qualifying spots: 4

Contest Rating:	5
Value Rating:	4
Qualifier Rating:	3 (Ratio – 50:1)

■

With its purse of $60,000 and its November spot on the annual tournament calendar, the Aqueduct Handicapping Challenge has become the premier fall handicapping contest in the East. This two-day event is guaranteed to sell out all 200 entries with no shortage of people willing to pay $300 to enter in pursuit of this contest's four qualifying spots in the DRF/NTRA National Handicapping Championship. The competition will be tough here because top players who have yet to qualify from both the New York area and other parts of the country will all be converging on this contest. Nevertheless, this is a highly recommended contest to play in if you still need to qualify, because Aqueduct pays back 100 percent of all entry fees in the form of prizes. The track also does a professional job of hosting the event with a constantly updated scoreboard and good customer service that includes freebies such as meals, programs, admission, parking, and a bonus gift.

The Aqueduct Handicapping Challenge format has players making 10 mythical bets a day on the races from Aqueduct and Churchill Downs. At least six of the 10 plays must be made on the live card. Nine of the 10 daily bets are $20 to win and $20 to place. The 10th bet on each day of the two-day event is a double-point best bet for $40 to win and $40 to place. The contest is worth $60,000 and pays down to 20th place with $25,000 going to the winner.

Why attend? This contest offers great value with Aqueduct paying back all entry fees to the winners and also kicking in several bonus freebies including those four coveted spots in the National Handicapping Championship. Players get an opportunity to test their skills against some of the best tournament players in the country. Fans of scoreboards at contests will love the fact that they will always know where they stand in relation to the rest of the field in this contest.

Why not? The competition is extremely tough in this tournament. Because it is late in the year, pro players from all over the country who have yet to qualify are flying in to compete. There are only two tracks open for play in this contest, Aqueduct and Churchill Downs, and more than half your bets must be made at Aqueduct after its turf-racing season has ended, so some of the fields can be relatively small. With a choice of so few races, many entrants end up picking the same "playable" events. Because of this format, it can be very difficult to win unless you catch some high-priced horses.

How to win: Spend the $600 and buy two entries to increase your chances of winning. It is especially important to use your two daily $40-to-win and $40-to-place wagers on horses with double-digit odds and to hit one or both of those bets. Aqueduct is filled with wise-guy bettors who know all the ins and outs at that track, and a little local knowledge can go a long way in this contest. It typically takes a total of just about $1,000 in mythical earnings in order to win and/or qualify for the National Handicapping Championship.

Where to stay: The best place to stay in the area of Aqueduct is in one of the nearby mega-hotels around JFK Airport. The **Sheraton JFK Airport Hotel** (718-489-1000) is one of the smaller and more inexpensive options, as is the **Courtyard by Marriott New York City/JFK Airport** (718-848-2121).

Where to eat: The place to go after the races at Aqueduct is **Don Peppe's** (135-158 Lefferts Blvd.; 718-845-7587), which serves heaping portions of family-style Italian food. Get there early or expect to wait, because Don Peppe's doesn't take reservations.

Contact info: Call NYRA at (718) 641-4700 ext. 734 and ask for information about their next handicapping contest.

BALLY'S SUMMER STAKES   *Recommended

Where: Bally's Las Vegas
When: Late July, early August
Who: 200 entries
How much: $1,000 entry fee (limit two per person)
Purse: $200,000
Scoreboard? No
DRF/NTRA qualifying spots: 4

Contest Rating: 5
Value Rating: 4
Qualifier Rating: 3 (Ratio – 50:1)

■

The Bally's Summer Stakes is one of the newest DRF/NTRA qualifying contests, and starting in January 2003, the Race and Sports Book at Bally's Las Vegas will host the National Handicapping Championship. The two-day contest costs $1,000 to enter and will offer a big purse of $200,000 based on a full field of 200 entries. All entry fees will be returned to the winners in the form of prize money and contestants who enter early also make themselves eligible for an "Out of the Gate" 10 percent bonus on all cash winnings during the contest.

Formerly, this contest was divided into two one-day segments including a win, place, show day and an exacta-wagering day. Bally's, however, is planning to change this format in favor of a more traditional two-day contest consisting of $2 win-and-place betting. For each winner selected in the contest, players will receive additional points besides the $2 win-and-place mutuel payoffs. This twist will be in place to reward players who pick a lot of winners, not just a lot of longshots. Six tracks will be open for betting in the contest including some combination of Arlington, Calder, Del Mar, Ellis, Laurel, Louisiana Downs, Monmouth, and Saratoga. All odds will be capped at 25-1 ($52) to win and 12-1 ($26) to place. The $200,000 total purse will be split into daily prize money and cumulative prize money.

Why attend? This contest does everything right. It pays back 100 percent of all entry fees in the form of prize money and even offers bonus money for early-bird sign-ups. The contest offers a wide selection of tracks to choose from, and features an innovative new point format that rewards players who pick winners, not longshots.

Why not? A $1,000 entry fee is too much for a large percentage of tournament players around the country.

How to win: This contest is one of just a couple now offering bonus points for every winner in addition to only giving points based on actual mutuel payoffs. This is an excellent idea that puts a premium on consistency as well as high-priced horses. Pick a lot of winners in this kind of contest, and you will be rewarded. Take the format into account, and try to focus on mid-priced horses instead of big bombs.

Where to stay: All contestants are eligible for a special Bally's Summer Stakes rate at **Bally's Las Vegas**. Why would you stay anywhere else?

Where to eat: You're in trouble if you can't find good food for any taste in Las Vegas. If you're staying at Bally's, try **Bally's Steakhouse**. This contest provides players with complementary breakfast, lunch, and cocktails in the Skyview Room on the 26th floor. On the Sunday morning after the contest, however, you might want to treat yourself to Bally's **Sterling Champagne Brunch**, which is worth every penny of its big price tag.

Contact info: Call 800-468-8946 to request information and an entry form, or go to *www.ballysraceandsports.com*.

BAY MEADOWS/DRF HANDICAPPING CHALLENGE

Where: Bay Meadows, San Mateo, California
When: September-October
Who: 4,000 entries expected
How much: Free
Purse: $5,000
Scoreboard? No
DRF/NTRA qualifying spots: 4

Contest Rating: 2
Value Rating: Free
Qualifier Rating: 1 (Ratio – 250:1)

■

Bay Meadows hosts a free contest during its fall meeting consisting of two preliminary rounds and a final round. Round One takes place over a three- or four-day period. Contestants pick up an entry blank and attempt to pick at least one show horse on any given day. Participants may play on more than one day if necessary, but can only earn one second-round entry per person. Successful handicappers (almost everyone) will then receive a letter inviting them to play in the second round four weeks later. For the second round, advancing players must select at least one place horse on the day's live race card. Players who are successful in Round Two (again, almost everyone) can then advance to the Bay Meadows final round. Again, players can earn only one final-round berth per person. In the final, qualifying players must try to select winners on Bay Meadows races 3 through 8. The players who amass the highest totals based on mythical $2 wagers will win trips to the DRF/NTRA National Handicapping Championship and split $5,000 in prize money.

Why attend? This is a free contest offering $5,000 in prize money and four qualifying spots in the National Handicapping Championship.

Why not? This contest requires three separate trips to Bay Meadows, but odds of earning a trip to Las Vegas are still slim with thousands of people likely to enter.

How to win: Simply show up for every round and you will dramatically improve your chances of winning. More entrants will be lost to attrition than through actually failing to qualify for the next round. There will probably be close to 1,000 players still around for the finals, so you had better think of a way to go 5 for 6 or 6 for 6 in order to have a chance to win.

Where to stay: A quality place to stay near the track is the **San Mateo Marriott** (650-653-6000). Another is the **Best Western/ Los Prados Inn** (650-341-3300).

Where to eat: Head toward downtown San Mateo for a good selection of places to eat and drink. A good sports bar is the **3rd Ave. Sports Bar & Grill** (77 E. 3rd Ave.; 650-340-9872). For a more upscale experience, head to **Bogie's Restaurant** (60 E. 3rd Ave.; 650-579-5911) for French and Italian cuisine with a Mediterranean twist.

Contact info: Call Bay Meadows at 650-573-RACE or dial 650-573-4617.

BELMONT PARK HANDICAPPING CHALLENGE   *Recommended

Where: Belmont Park, Elmont, New York
When: July
Who: Limited to 200 entries (up to two entries per person)
How much: $300 entry fee
Purse: $60,000
Scoreboard? Yes, every bet for every player
DRF/NTRA qualifying spots: 4

Contest Rating: 5
Value Rating: 4
Qualifier Rating: 3 (Ratio – 50:1)

■

A stellar field of handicapping-tournament notables is always on hand for Belmont Park's Handicapping Challenge. The two-day event sells out its 200 spots every year at a big price tag of $300 a pop. The contest allows players to pay for two entries, and many do so for three reasons: 1) Belmont pays back 100 percent of all entry fees in the form of prize money; 2) Belmont offers four qualifying spots in the DRF/NTRA National Handicapping Championship; and 3) Belmont does an excellent job hosting this contest, which includes a constantly updated scoreboard and freebies on meals, programs, admission, parking, and a bonus gift (such as a hat or golf shirt).

Players make 10 mythical bets a day on the races from Belmont and Monmouth Park, with at least six of the 10 plays on the live card. Nine of the 10 daily bets are $20 to win and $20 to place, but Belmont throws in a twist to its format by adding a 10th double-points best bet for $40 to win and $40 to place on each day of the two-day event. The contest is worth $60,000 and pays down to 20th place with $25,000 going to the winner.

Why attend? This contest offers great value with Belmont paying back all entry fees to the winners and also kicking in several bonus freebies including those four coveted spots in the National Handicapping Championship. Players get an opportunity to square off against some of the biggest names on the tournament circuit in the comfort of the Marquis Tent at beautiful Belmont Park during one of the best race meets of the year.

Why not? This is a tough contest to win with so many big-name handicappers in attendance. The only other negative is the lack of choices as far as simulcast races are concerned. Players basically end up focusing on the same "playable" races at Belmont and then have only one to four plays remaining to use at Monmouth, the contest's only other track.

How to win: Two entries are allowed in this contest, so go ahead and pony up the $600 and increase your odds considerably. Since there are not a lot of different races to choose from in this contest, it becomes very important to win with some of the highest-priced horses. It is especially important to hit at least one of your daily $40-to-win and $40-to-place wagers on a longshot in the 10-1 range (or higher). It typically takes more than $1,000 to win and/or qualify for the National Handicapping Championship. In last year's contest, winner William Jackson hit one of his $40-and-$40 plays on a $21.80 winner and eventually finished with over $1,100 in his bankroll. All top-four finishers, and only the top four finishers, in the contest's 2002 renewal totaled over $1,000.

Where to stay: The closest and most convenient hotel to Belmont Park is the **Floral Park Motor Lodge** (800-255-9680), which offers 107 rooms and is located just minutes from the track on busy Jericho Turnpike.

Where to eat: After the races at Belmont Park, everyone heads to **Trinity Restaurant** (190 Jericho Turnpike; 516-358-5584) in neighboring Floral Park for its lively bar scene and some of the best Irish pub-grub on Long Island. Trinity also features daily specials including tasty pastas and fish dishes.

Contact info: Call NYRA at (516) 488-6000 ext. 734 and ask for information about their next handicapping contest.

BETTOR RACING OTB MIDWEST CLASSIC   *Recommended

Where: Bettor Racing OTB in Sioux Falls, South Dakota
When: A Saturday in between the Preakness and Belmont Stakes
Who: Due to space restrictions, the contest is limited to 50 players and 100 entries.
How much: Entry fee is $250
Purse: About $20,000 based on 80 entries.
Scoreboard? Majority rules
DRF/NTRA qualifying spots: 4

Contest Rating: 5
Value Rating: 4
Qualifier Rating: 5 (Ratio – 12.5:1)

The Bettor Racing OTB is a small betting shop located in Sioux Falls, South Dakota. The OTB's owner is J. Randy Gallo, a high roller with a penchant for the pick six who qualified for the first two DRF/NTRA National Handicapping Championships. Gallo, an avid traveling tournament player, is well known by many of the top handicappers in the country and has enough pull to get them up to Sioux Falls to play in his contest. The result is an annual all-star event consisting of dozens of big players from around the country who specialize in playing in and winning big-money handicapping tournaments.

The Bettor Racing OTB Midwest Classic is a one-day contest with $20,000 and four qualifying slots to the DRF/NTRA National Handicapping Championship hanging in the balance. A maximum of 50 players can enter the contest, but with two entries allowed per person, as many as 100 entries could be accepted. Keep in mind, however, that players cannot qualify for the National Handicapping Championship twice. Therefore, 50 players compete for four DRF/NTRA qualifying spots for an excellent ratio of 12.5:1.

Players make mythical $2 win-and-place bets on a total of 12 races from five different tracks, and all winning payoffs are capped at 20-1 to win ($42), and 10-1 to place ($22). The players who accumulate the highest bankrolls based on their $2 win and $2 place wagers are the winners. The contest pays off 100 percent of all entry fees in the form of prizes. The contest pays back 10 places with 40 percent of the pot, or roughly $8,000, going to the winner.

Why attend? In order to be the best, you have to beat the best. Aside from the National Handicapping Championship, this is perhaps the best tournament field of the year. Unlike the NHC, however, you don't have to qualify in order to test your skills against the best in the game. The contest is well run with a personal touch, and your numerical chance of qualifying for the national championship in this contest is very good at just over 12-1. Last but not least, this contest pays 100 percent of all entry fees back to the players in the form of prize money.

Why not? The field size is always small, but very select, so don't fool yourself into thinking this contest will be easy to win. In reality, the competition doesn't get any tougher than in this tournament. The 2002 renewal of this event drew all three past winners of the DRF/NTRA national championship—Steven Walker (2000), Judy Wagner (2001), and Herman Miller (2002). If you're not much of a traveler, this contest might not be for you. Sioux Falls is not a convenient place to get to. Entrants are faced with either a long drive or a flight with several stopovers or connections from just about everywhere in the country.

How to win: Based on previous results, it's going to take a total of around $120 to win this contest, and a total near $100 for a top-four finish and a DRF/NTRA qualifying spot. With just a dozen $2 win-and-place bets at your disposal, you can't win this contest playing $4 to $6 horses. Even $8 horses (3-1) are not going to cut the mustard since you'd need to hit roughly nine 3-1 horses in order to reach the $100 to $120 level. Play horses above 5-1 odds and shoot for at least one cap horse (20-1 to win, 10-1 place), which will add $64 to your bankroll. You'll be going against some of the sharpest players in the country, so you'll need some big-priced horses in order to win.

Where to stay: The Bettor Racing OTB sets up special tournament rates at several local hotels. To stay close to the facility, book a room at the **Holiday Inn City Centre** (605-339-2000). Those who want a location more convenient to the airport should stay at the **Ramada Inn Airport** (605-336-1020).

Where to eat: For fine dining in Sioux Falls, head to **Minerva's** (301 S. Phillips Ave.; 605-334-0386) for great steaks and pasta. For pizza and other casual fare, check out **Theo's Great Food** (601 W. 33rd St.; 605-338-6801).

Contact info: Call the Bettor Racing OTB at (888) 299-9861 and ask for general manager Ray Henry.

BRADLEY TELETHEATER'S AUTOTOTE HANDICAPPING CHALLENGE
*Recommended

Where: Bradley Teletheater, Windsor Locks, Connecticut (Hartford area)
When: July
Who: Field fills up at 225 entries
How much: $300 entry fee
Purse: $68,000
Scoreboard? Yes, every bet by every player is charted
DRF/NTRA qualifying spots: 2

Contest Rating:	5
Value Rating:	4
Qualifier Rating:	2 (Ratio – 112:1)

■

The Bradley Teletheater Handicapping Challenge is the slightly younger and smaller sibling of Autotote's other annual handicapping event, the Sports Haven Handicapping Challenge. This contest, along with the one at Sports Haven, has become the East's premier tournament with accomplished players coming from all four corners of the country in order to participate against the best of the best.

The Handicapping Challenge is a two-day event involving the race cards from three tracks—Belmont, Hollywood, and Monmouth. Players make 10 mythical $200 wagers on each day of the contest. Betting is win, place, and/or show, and must be in $50 increments (example: $100 to win, $50 to place, $50 to show). All winning payoffs are capped at 20-1 to win, 10-1 to place, and 5-1 to show. The contest pays down to 20 places with 30 percent of the pot ($20,000) going to the winner. The contest returns 100 percent of all entry fees in the form of prizes, and the top four finishers all qualify for the National Handicapping Championship.

Why attend? This is a professionally run, prestigious midsummer event that gives entrants a chance to measure their skills against the best in the game. Prize money is good, but yet not too top-heavy with the top 20 finishers all getting paid no less than $400 (all of the top 14 get no less than $1,000). The contest offers plenty of perks like complimentary *Daily Racing Forms*, food, and freebies, and still pays back 100 percent of all entry fees in the form of prize money.

Why not? The ratio of entries to qualifiers (112:1) isn't bad, but don't expect an easy road into the national finals in this contest. You'll be going up against some serious players who know what they're doing.

How to win: In order to build a total high enough, a winning player is going to need to bet his whole $200 to win on each race, while also taking aim at plenty of longshots hovering around the 20-1 odds cap. Don't bet horses lower than 4-1 or 5-1 unless it is a strategic maneuver, and always be sure to take advantage of the scoreboard late in the contest and adjust your wagering accordingly.

Past winners of this contest have totaled $10,220 (Ed Fountaine, 1998), $11,160 (David Crupi, 1999), $11,310 (John Gilberg, 2000), $10,720 (Mike Labriola, 2001), and $13,700 (Tom Quigley, 2002). The winning average of $11,422 means you should shoot for something around that amount if you hope to have a chance to win. The top four finishers qualify for the National Handicapping Championship, and $10,000 has generally been enough for a top-four finish with the exception of 2002, when 15 players topped $10,000 and $12,860 was necessary to qualify.

Where to stay: Nearby hotels offering special reduced contest rates include the **Ramada Inn** (860-623-9494), and the **Double Tree Inn** (860-627-5171).

Where to eat: When Saturday's action ends everyone heads to **Albert's American Restaurant** (159 Ella T. Grasso Turnpike; 860-292-6801), which is just down the road from the Bradley Teletheater. You may also want to go 11 miles south to Hartford for a trip to **Coach's Sports Bar & Grille** (187 Allyn St.; 860-522-6224), which is owned by UConn men's basketball coach Jim Calhoun.

Contact info: Call 203-946-3140 or 203-946-3139 for more information.

CAL EXPO HANDICAPPING CONTEST

Where: Cal Expo (Sacramento) and six participating branches including Santa Clara, Santa Rosa (The Jockey Club), Vallejo (Sonoma Fair), Pleasanton, San Joaquin Fair (Winners), and Big Fresno Fair (Clue One).

When: August

Who: Approximately 700 entries. Close to 100 entrants compete at each preliminary site.

How much: Free

Purse: $2,000

Scoreboard? Yes, in the final round

DRF/ NTRA qualifying spots: 4

Contest Rating:	3
Value Rating:	Free
Qualifier Rating:	2 (Ratio – 175:1)

■

The California State Fair (Cal Expo) contest consists of both on-track and off-track preliminary rounds plus a final round held one week later at the Cal Expo races in Sacramento. A total of seven outlets participate, with each sending their top four finishers to compete in the one-day 28-player final round at Cal Expo. The top four finishers in the final round all qualify for the DRF/NTRA National Handicapping Championship final in Las Vegas.

Participants can pick up entry blanks on the day of the contest, and then must try to select the winners of Cal Expo races 4 through 9 on the day of the preliminary round. Contest winners will be the players who amass the highest totals based on mutuel win prices and a bonus of five points per winner. For example, if you pick a $10 winner, you get 10 points plus a 5-point bonus for a total of 15 points. If you pick a $30 winner, you get 30 points plus a 5-point bonus. All payoffs are capped at $50 (24-1). Rules of the Cal Expo final round are the same as the preliminaries. The final-round winner gets a $500 cash prize, with $350 for second, $350 for third, $200 for fourth, and $100 each for places fifth through 10th.

Why attend? If you live in Northern California, you shouldn't need to drive far to enter this contest at any one of seven preliminary sites. The contest costs nothing to enter, and you will only need to finish in the top four among a field of just 28 players if you are fortunate enough to make it to the Cal Expo final round.

Why not? Odds are against you qualifying for the national finals in this contest. You should expect as many as 100 players to enter the preliminary round at each of the seven sites for a total of 700 players. Out of that original 700 people, only four will eventually qualify for the National Handicapping Championship. Finishing in the top four out of roughly 100 players at your preliminary site is not enough to guarantee you a spot in the national finals. You'll still need a top-four finish the following week in this contest's final round at Cal Expo.

How to win: The first thing you can do to upgrade your odds is to enter a preliminary that is slightly off the beaten track and therefore likely to attract fewer entrants. Sacramento and Fresno probably will have the biggest fields, so go elsewhere if you can. The format of this contest puts a premium on picking winners, slightly downgrading the value of longshots by adding five bonus points (dollars) to the value of every winning horse. Suddenly, a 5-1 horse is worth $17 instead of just $12. Try to pick the most winners you can, regardless of price, and take advantage of all the bonus money you can get.

Where to stay: Several area hotels offer special discounted rates if you mention you're visiting the California State Fair. **Comfort Inn & Suites** (916-379-0400) is 10 minutes from Cal Expo. **The Best Western Expo Inn** (916-929-8772) is also close by. Call the individual preliminary sites in Santa Clara, Santa Rosa, Vallejo, Pleasanton, San Joaquin, and Fresno for more local information.

Where to eat: There are hundreds of food stands at the **California State Fair** grounds in Sacramento. Try the onion rings and fried calamari at **Milo's Fish and Chips** or the beef ribs and tri-tip sandwich at **TFC's Barbecue** stand.

Contact info: Call (916) 263-3044 or (916) 263-3279 for details.

CANTERBURY PARK'S DOG DAYS OF SUMMER HANDICAPPING TOURNAMENT

Where: Canterbury Park, Shakopee, Minnesota (Minneapolis area)
When: August
Who: 60 entries (maximum of two entries per person)
How much: $100 entry fee plus a $400 live, real-money bankroll
Purse: $5,500 based on 60 entries, plus players keep their bankroll earnings
Scoreboard? Yes, occasional updates
DRF/NTRA qualifying spots: 2

Contest Rating:	3
Value Rating:	4
Qualifier Rating:	4 (Ratio – 30:1)

■

The Dog Days of Summer Handicapping Tournament at Canterbury Park is a two-day event that has been held at the track every August since 1997. Players pay a $100 entry fee which goes toward the purse, and then must purchase a $400 account-wagering card that serves as an entrant's live, real-money bankroll throughout the contest. Players can wager their $400 bankroll however they want on any track and any pool (exotics included) they please in order to increase their total. Entrants must bet a minimum of $100 on each day of the contest, but there is no maximum, meaning the whole $400 plus earnings on that amount can be bet and re-bet as few or as many times as you like. The top two finishers qualify for the National Handicapping Championship, and the top three earn prize money with $2,500 for first, $1,500 for second, and $1,000 for third. The day-one leader also receives $500.

    * Canterbury Park also hosts two other qualifying contests during the year, each with one DRF/NTRA qualifying spot available. The first is the Road to Kentucky Handicapping Tournament, a 14-week marathon designed primarily to give local players a free shot at competing for $50,000 and a qualifying spot in the National Handicapping Championship. The multi-week event begins over the winter and follows

the trail of Kentucky Derby prep races through the spring until its culmination with the Derby itself on the first Saturday in May.

*Canterbury Park's fourth and final DRF/NTRA qualifying slot goes to the winner of a one-day October contest with an inexpensive $30 entry fee. Players in that event make 10 $2 win and $2 place bets for all the marbles. The October contest is limited to 100 entries, and offers a purse of $3,000 based on a full field.

Why attend? This tournament is just like real-life betting, so if you're going to the track that weekend, you might as well go to Canterbury Park. This contest allows only 60 entries, and players can enter more than once, meaning that the odds of landing one of the two available DRF/NTRA qualifying spots are relatively good. Canterbury's winter-spring Road to Kentucky Tournament is a great value for local players who can be at the track every Saturday. The track puts up $50,000 of its own money and you don't have to pay a dime to take a shot at your share of the loot.

Why not? This tournament is more of a betting contest than a handicapping contest. It is difficult to strategize for this event, because almost anything is possible due to the unstructured format and the acceptance of exotic bets.

How to win: It's almost impossible to know how much money you'll need to win this tournament; however, we do know that the last three winners (2000-2002) totaled $2,930, $2,400, and $1,770. You can attempt to play a bunch of races and hammer out a solid profit over the course of the two-day contest, but a better strategy is probably to find one good 5-1 to 10-1 shot and bet your entire bankroll. Stay alive on Day One of the contest by betting your daily minimum of $100 to show. Then take whatever you have left and try to connect on a tap-out bet on Day Two. This was the strategy used by 2000 winner James Stagle of St. Paul, Minnesota, who won the tournament with a bankroll of $2,930, which he earned by cashing a $425 win bet on a horse paying $13.80.

Where to stay: There are three hotels located in Shakopee within a mile of Canterbury Park including the **Country Inn & Suites** (952-445-0200), **Park Inn & Suites** (952-445-3644), and **AmericInn** (952-445-6775).

Where to eat: A nice upscale place to eat in Shakopee is **Dangerfield's Restaurant** (1583 1st Ave.; 952-445-2245). For good, cheap eats and drinks, there's also **Saba's Sports Bar & Grill** (911 1st Ave.; 952-496-9044). If you want lunch in the area at someplace besides the racetrack, try **Wampach's diner** (126 1st Ave.; 952-445-2721).

Contact info: Call Canterbury Park at 952-496-6437.

CHURCHILL DOWNS SPRING/FALL HANDICAPPING CONTESTS

Where: Churchill Downs, Louisville, Kentucky
When: Wednesdays during the spring and fall live race meets
Who: Each day limited to 350 entries
How much: $20 per week
Purse: $13,000 each contest (spring and fall)
Scoreboard? Yes
DRF/NTRA qualifying spots: 2 contests, 2 qualifiers per contest

Contest Rating:	3
Value Rating:	3
Qualifier Rating:	2 (Ratio – 175:1)

■

Churchill Downs hosts month-long handicapping contests during its spring and fall meets to determine a total of four qualifiers to the DRF/NTRA National Handicapping Championship (two winners in the spring, two in the fall). The contests are held at the track on consecutive Wednesdays, with four preliminaries leading to a one-day final round held on the last Wednesday of the meet. Weekly entry fee is $20, and players compete for $2,000 in weekly prize money and an invitation to the final round where $5,000 in prize money and the two qualifying spots will be at stake. Each weekly winner will earn $700, and payouts will be made down to eighth place. Also, the top 15 weekly finishers will qualify for Churchill's final round. The overall winner earns $2,000 and a trip to the national finals in Las Vegas. The runner-up earns a $1,000 second prize and also qualifies.

The Churchill Downs contests used to feature a $500 mythical-bankroll format, with players attempting to earn as much money as possible on the live races based on win, place, show, and exacta wagers. This format was changed, however, for the 2002 fall meet. In order to stay more uniform with the rules of the national finals, entrants now are asked to make mythical $2-to-win and $2-to-place wagers on the Churchill Downs live card.

Why attend? The weekly contests are only $20 to enter, and still give you a chance at some decent prize money. If you can advance to the Churchill Downs final round, your chances of qualifying for Las Vegas increase to 30-1 since you need to be one of the top two finishers in a final round field of 60 players.

Why not? As many as 350 players could show up for any given weekly contest, and only the top 15 each week advance to Churchill Downs' final round. Even if you do advance, you are not guaranteed of winning. The more players that enter this contest, the bigger the takeout will be. Not all money that comes in as entry fees will go out as prize money.

How to win: Since the format was changed recently, there really aren't any past results to use as a guide. However, since the new contest involves the familiar $2-to-win and $2-to-place format, you can count on at least needing to double your original bankroll in order to win.

Where to stay: For an inexpensive spot close to the airport, stay at the **Hampton Inn Louisville-Airport** (502-366-8100). Two favorites downtown include the **Galt House** (502-589-5200) and the **Seelbach Hilton** (502-585-3200).

Where to eat: Whether you're heading to Louisville for a handicapping contest, the Kentucky Derby, or whatever, be sure to stop by **Molly Malone's Irish Pub** (933 Baxter Ave.; 502-473-1222) on the Bardstown Road strip. Say hello to owner Tadghe O'Callaghan, the brother of trainer Niall O'Callaghan. Two places racetrackers like to go in the Frankfurt Avenue area include **Porcini** (2730 Frankfurt Ave.; 502-894-8686) for Italian food, and **Furlongs** (2350 Frankfurt Ave.; 502-896-6210), a racing-themed Cajun restaurant. There are also some good places in downtown Louisville including **Vincenzo's Italian Restaurant** (150 S. 5th St.; 502-580-1350), and **Kuntz's Fourth & Market** (115 S. Fourth St.; 502-585-5555).

Contact info: Call the Churchill Downs promotions department at 502-636-4452.

COLONIAL DOWNS HANDICAPPING CONTEST

Where: Colonial Downs, New Kent County, Virginia
When: During the live Colonial Downs meet (June-July)
Who: Field is limited to 200 players (one entry per person)
How much: Entry fee is $100
Purse: $10,000 guaranteed goes to the top four finishers
Scoreboard? Yes.
DRF/NTRA qualifying spots: 4

Contest Rating:	3
Value Rating:	2
Qualifier Rating:	3 (Ratio – 50:1)

■

The Colonial Downs Handicapping Contest is a one-day event held at Colonial Downs, which is located in central Virginia, halfway between Richmond and Williamsburg. The contest takes place in the track's Sky Suites and Ballroom located on the fourth floor, and revolves around the day's live race card from Colonial Downs. As many as 200 players will vie for $10,000 in prizes and four qualifying spots in the DRF/NTRA National Handicapping Championship.

The format of the contest is similar in some ways to the format of the national finals in Las Vegas. Players will make mythical $2 win and $2 place wagers (same horse) on the full card from Colonial Downs, excluding steeplechase races. Odds are capped at 20-1 to win ($42), and 10-1 to place ($22), and the top four finishers based on actual mutuel payoffs will split the entire purse and the four DRF/NTRA qualifying spots. Prize money is $10,000 with $5,000 going to the winner, $2,500 to second, $1,500 to third, and $1,000 for fourth.

Why attend? Local everyday players, or players familiar with racing at Colonial Downs, will have an advantage in this contest, because the betting takes place exclusively on live races from Colonial Downs. There are excellent prizes to shoot for as long as you finish in the top four.

Why not? A full field of 200 players would put $20,000 into the pot (200 x $100), but the payout is set at only $10,000, so there could be as much as 50 percent takeout in this contest based on the maximum number of entries. This means the contest is only a good value if 100 or fewer people enter. Local fans with track knowledge only are encouraged to play this event, because it involves strictly live races and no simulcasts. Finally, this contest is very top heavy, with only the top four finishers in a field of up to 200 earning all of the prize money. That means the odds against you leaving with something to show for your hard work are 50-1.

How to win: If you follow the racing at Colonial on a daily basis, your odds of winning should increase considerably. Also, horseplayers who favor turf racing could have an advantage here because Colonial Downs runs such a high percentage of its races on grass. Since this contest involves only one track (Colonial), stabbing at longshots may not be as important as plugging away with winners race after race. Pick your spots. Just keep in mind, however, that it will be very difficult to beat 196 other players unless you are one of the few people in the contest who hits the highest-priced winner on the card.

The winner of the 2002 Colonial Downs contest, Taylor Jones of Richmond, Virginia, hit six winners and a second to total $119.80. However, it took a final bankroll of only $71.20 in order to finish fourth and qualify for the DRF/NTRA finals.

Where to stay: The best places to stay are about 17 miles down the road toward the west near the Richmond airport. **The Richmond Airport Microtel Inn and Suites** (804-737-3322) is a good choice, as is the **Holiday Inn Richmond-Airport** (804-222-6450), which offers a $69 rate.

Where to eat: Unless you want to drive to Richmond to eat, try the **White House Restaurant** (3560 N. Courthouse Rd.; 804-966-9700) which is four miles from Colonial Downs in Providence Forge. Also in Providence Forge is **Jones & Hawkes Southern Style Restaurant** (7801 Pocahontas Trail; 804-966-1325).

Contact info: Call for contest information at (804) 966-7223 ext. 1021.

DELAWARE PARK HANDICAPPING TOURNAMENT

Where: Delaware Park, Stanton, Delaware
When: June and October
Who: Tournament is "limited" to 300 entries, but 315 entered June 2002 contest
How much: Entry fee of $100 plus $200 real-money bankroll
Purse: $30,000 based on 300 entries
Scoreboard? No
DRF/NTRA qualifying spots: 2 in each contest

Contest Rating: 3
Value Rating: 4
Qualifier Rating: 2 (Ratio – 150:1)

■

Delaware Park hosts two tournaments a year to determine its four qualifiers to the National Handicapping Championship. The tournaments are real-money events, where players pay a $100 entry fee and then bet with their own $200 cash betting stake in an effort to accumulate the highest bankroll in the one-day event. All players keep their parimutuel earnings. The tournament is also tied in to Delaware's Player's Club, so participants with enough points can use those points to enter the contest in lieu of the $100 entry fee.

In the contest, players must bet a minimum of 10 races during the day with no maximum. There is a minimum bet of $20 per race, ensuring that a player's $200 bankroll will be bet at least once during the contest. All bets must be win, place, or show on a large selection of tracks likely to include Belmont, Churchill, Monmouth, Pimlico, Philadelphia Park, and of course the live card from Delaware Park. The top two finishers based on mutuel earnings at the end of each tournament will qualify for the DRF/NTRA National Handicapping Championship. The top 50 finishers also receive prize money, with half the pool, or about $15,000, going to the winner. Places 11 through 50 get their $100 entry fee back.

Why attend? This is a great competition that closely mirrors a real day of betting at the racetrack. The fact that real money is involved limits a large amount of the stabbing at longshots that is often so prevalent at mythical-money contests. Win or lose, you get to keep whatever money you have left at the end of the day. Unlike so many contests, this tournament isn't top heavy. The top 50 of the 300 entrants will win at least $100 at the end of the day.

Why not? Chances of qualifying for the National Handicapping Championship are slim. With a field of 300 players in each of Delaware's two contests, the ratio of players to qualifiers is 150:1 based on just two qualifying spots in each tournament.

How to win: Somebody usually freaks in this contest, blowing away the rest of the competition with a final total between $2,000 and $2,500. That's one heckuva day at the track when you consider those bankrolls were built with only straight bets. Figure on needing to turn your $200 into over $1,500 for a top-two finish and a shot to qualify. There is really no one best way to do this, but I recommend trying to bump up your bankroll with some winners early in the contest, and then swinging for the fences with larger bets once your bankroll has grown to a decent level. Since you must make 10 bets, you could also try to tread water through your first nine bets and then bet everything you have in the contest on one 10-1 shot for all the marbles. Generally speaking, if you get your $200 back by the end of the contest, you'll probably have enough money to finish in the top 50 and get your entry fee back. However, why end the contest with $200 left on your tab when a last-minute $200 bet on a 10-1 winner could land you in the National Handicapping Championship?

Where to stay: Call and ask for a special rate at Delaware Park's host hotel, the **Cristiana Hilton** (302-631-1558), which is described as a "country manor" near downtown Wilmington. For a location more convenient to the track, try the **Red Roof Inn** (I-95 and Route 7; 302-292-2870) just down the road from the back gate.

Where to eat: If you can find it, **Kid Shelleens** (14th and Scott Streets, Wilmington; 302-658-4600) is a lively grill and bar with great outdoor patio seating. For steaks, make the drive to **Sullivan's Steakhouse** in Wilmington (5525 Concord Pike in the Market Square shopping center; 302-479-7970).

Contact info: Call (302) 994-2521 ext. 7136 to ask for information on the next tournament.

DEL MAR DRF HANDICAPPING CHALLENGE

Where: Del Mar Thoroughbred Club, Del Mar, California
When: July-September live meet
Who: All on-track and on-line customers
How much: Contests are free to enter
Purse: $20,000
Scoreboard? Final round only
DRF/NTRA qualifying spots: 3 on-track, 1 on-line

Contest Rating: 3
Value Rating: Free
Qualifier Rating: 1 (Ratio – 2,500:1)

■

Del Mar hosts two contests—one on-track and one on-line—during its seven-week live Thoroughbred meet beginning in late July. Both contests are free to enter.

The main contest is the on-track version, and it consists of three rounds. All on-track patrons on the opening weekend of the meet are invited to fill out an entry blank for the first round of the contest. Players are asked to pick one horse to show in races 4 through 9 on the live race card. Anyone who picks even a single in-the-money finisher in any of the day's six designated races will be sent an entry blank for Round Two of the contest three weeks later. In Round Two, returning players fill out their entry blanks with mythical $2-to-win and $2-to-place picks on races 4 through 9 at Del Mar. The top 20 finishers in Round Two based on total mutuel earnings will advance to Del Mar's final round on the last Sunday of the meet. The 20 finalists then compete against one another in a traditional $2-to-win, $2-to-place contest to determine three DRF/NTRA National Handicapping Championship qualifiers. Del Mar will supply a total of $2,000 in prizes for each preliminary day, and another $14,000 in prizes for the final round with $10,000 going to the winner.

In the separate on-line contest, players sign up and receive a mythical $100-per-race, per-day bankroll to win, place, or show only on each day of the 43-day Del Mar meet. There is an odds cap of 35-1 on all wagers. The player who accumulates the highest total for the meet wins Del Mar's fourth and final DRF/NTRA qualifying spot.

Why attend? Del Mar's contests are free to enter, so if you're at the track you might as well take a shot. It is extremely easy to advance from Round One into Round Two, but the field is likely to be narrowed down considerably in the second round due to no-shows. If you happen to have a good day at the races in Round Two, you may qualify for Del Mar's final round, where only 20 players will vie for three spots in the national finals (odds of 6.66-to-1).

Why not? If you have to travel to get to Del Mar, the on-track contest may not be for you. You must be at the track on three different weekends if you are lucky enough to keep advancing. Therefore, if you know you won't be able to make multiple trips to Del Mar during its July-September meet, you may as well stay home.

How to win: Nearly everyone who signs up will advance to the second round, so the contest basically begins in Round Two when the $2-to-win, $2-to-place format kicks in on Del Mar's races 4 through 9. This only gives you six races to separate yourself from your competition, so you had better be thinking price horses, and a lot of them. Don't be afraid to take some easy money on a sure winner, but if you do, balance out your ticket with some horses above 5-1 and 10-1 odds. In the on-line contest, you can only help your chances by logging on to the contest every day at *www.delmarracing.com*. You don't need to bet every day, but it helps to at least check the standings and plan your strategy.

Where to stay: Courtyard by Marriott (858-792-8200), technically located in Solana Beach, is probably the closest and most convenient hotel to the track. Slightly smaller budgets might prefer the **Best Western Stratford Inn** (858-755-1501) in Del Mar.

Where to eat: The Brigantine restaurant (3263 Camino Del Mar; 858-481-1166) is almost synonymous with Del Mar. The back patio of "The Brig" overlooks the far turn and is a great place to go for steaks, seafood, clam chowder, or just drinks at the expansive bar. Horsemen often head to **Red Tracton's** (550 Via De La Valle; 858-755-6600), which is "just a stone's throw from Del Mar." The Mexican food in the area is worth having, so head over to **En Fuego** (1314 Camino Del Mar; 858-792-6551). For fine dining and wild people-watching, take a 15-minute drive to **Cafe Japengo** (8960 University Center Lane; 858-450-3355) in La Jolla.

Contact info: Call 858-755-1141 ext. 3427 and ask for information, or log on to *www.delmarracing.com*.

ELLIS PARK-DRF/NTRA NATIONAL HANDICAPPING CHAMPIONSHIP CONTEST

Where: Ellis Park Race Course, Henderson, Kentucky
When: Three contests from July to August
Who: Expect fields of between 50 to 75 players in each contest
How much: Entry fee is either $75 for a single contest or $200 for all three
Purse: $1,550 for each contest
Scoreboard? Yes
DRF/NTRA qualifying spots: 4 total between three contests

Contest Rating:	3
Value Rating:	2
Qualifier Rating:	5 (Ratio – 25:1)

■

Ellis Park holds three separate contests during its summer meet to determine its four qualifiers to the DRF/NTRA National Handicapping Championship. The four spots in the finals go to the three individual contest winners and a fourth player with the highest combined point total in all three contests. Anywhere from 50 to 75 players usually enter each contest, with a large amount of the same players participating in all three. In total, roughly 100 different players are likely to play in one or more of the events, meaning that one in every 25 or so entrants will earn a trip to Las Vegas in this contest.

Players get to make 10 mythical $2 win and $2 place bets on the live 10-race card from Ellis Park. Win and place wagers do not have to be on the same horse. There has not been an odds cap in years past, but one is expected to be added beginning in 2003. The top 10 finishers in each contest earn prize money with $500 for first place, $300 for second, $200 for third, $100 for fourth, and $75 for fifth through tenth.

Why attend? This contest is worth entering if you can be at Ellis Park for all three editions. This gives you three chances to win a contest and another chance to qualify based on the highest accumulated total for all three contests. If you enter all three, the price per contest is only $66.66.

Why not? There are a few negatives involved in this competition, the biggest of which is a high takeout. Even with an entry fee of only $75, the track is likely to take in something in the neighborhood of $14,000 to $15,000 between all three contests. However, total prize money adds up to only $4,650 ($1,550 x 3). This means you will be going up against roughly a 66 percent takeout. Then again, if you're playing in this contest, you're probably in it for those four coveted DRF/NTRA qualifying spots more than anything, and the value of those trips to Las Vegas nearly tips the scales back in the players' favor.

How to win: First and foremost, show up at all three contests and you immediately increase your odds of winning Ellis Park's fourth qualifying spot, which goes to the player with the highest combined earnings for all three contests. This competition involves only live races, and everyone must bet every race on the live card from Ellis Park. Even with the addition of an odds cap, this format places a huge importance on hitting the highest-priced winner(s) on the card in order to win. You just can't let a longshot winner get past you and still have a chance to win, and you can't land a longshot unless you play longshots. Aim for horses at 5-1 odds or higher and swing for the fences when appropriate. Take advantage of the rule that says your win and place wagers don't have to be on the same horse.

Where to stay: The closest rooms to Ellis Park are at **Monica's 8 Motel** (270-827-9144). If you prefer a national chain, travel a little farther down Highway 41 to the **Comfort Inn** (270-827-8191), or the **Holiday Inn Express** (270-889-0533), where Ellis Park fans can receive discounted stays.

Where to eat: **Wolf's Restaurant and Tavern** (31 N. Green St.; 270-826-5221) has been around since 1878 and is a solid choice for drinks and dinner. This part of the country is known for its barbecue, and **Greg's Bar-B-Q** is a good place to go for take-out ribs, chicken, and the like. For Mexican food, make a run for the border at **Los Toribio's** (2810 U.S. Highway 41 N.; 270-830-6610).

Contact info: Call 812-425-1456 and ask for Robert Cunningham for details.

EMERALD DOWNS' ULTIMATE QUALIFYING TOURNAMENT *Recommended

Where: Emerald Downs, Auburn, Washington
When: July
Who: Limited to 400 entries
How much: Free
Purse: $11,600
Scoreboard? Limited updates
DRF/NTRA qualifying spots: 12

Contest Rating:	5
Value Rating:	Free
Qualifier Rating:	4 (Ratio – 33:1)

■

Emerald Downs unveiled this contest in July 2002, becoming the first venue ever to offer 12 DRF/NTRA National Handicapping Championship qualifying spots in a single tournament. Tracks and OTB's pay dues to the NTRA in order to send one group of four qualifiers to the national championship, but Emerald is willing to go the extra mile for their guests by paying triple the amount and sending three teams of four to the NHC. Making the Ultimate Qualifying Tournament even more attractive to potential players is the fact that, despite prize money of $11,600 and a list of free amenities, the contest is free to enter and limited to the first 400 entries. The winner receives $10,000 in cash and another $500 in casino chips in Las Vegas along with the added perk of a room upgrade to a hotel suite at the host property of the National Handicapping Championship. The second- through 12th-place finishers all receive expense-paid trips to the national finals plus $100 in casino chips.

The format of the Ultimate Qualifying Tournament includes mythical $2 win and $2 place wagers on 15 races, including mandatory bets on the full card from Emerald Downs. The remaining five plays can be selected from a variety of simulcast tracks including Arlington, Calder, Del Mar, Ellis, and Saratoga. Odds are capped at 20-1 to win and 10-1 to place.

Note: Find out when Emerald begins taking entries for this event and contact them immediately on that day. Emerald reserved all 400 spots in its 2002 contest on the day they became available.

Why attend? This contest offers the kind of value that tournament players are looking for. Emerald Downs is offering 12 big

DRF/NTRA qualifying spots plus prize money and they aren't charging a dime for it. Even with the maximum number of 400 entrants, the ratio of players to qualifiers (33:1) is still very good.

Why not? This contest scores the top rating of five, so if you want to qualify for the DRF/NTRA National Handicapping Championship, there really is no reason not to give it a shot.

How to win: Learn a little something about the racing at Emerald Downs because two-thirds of the races in the contest will be from the live card there. If you've read this book and know a little something about tournament strategy, you'll have a strong edge on much of the competition and a good shot at a top-12 finish.

The winner of the 2002 Ultimate Tournament, David Brown of Wenatchee, Washington, totaled $181. With 12 qualifying spots on the line, however, it takes far less than that in order to qualify. Second place in 2002 was $150, and any total over $120 gives you a great chance to make it to Las Vegas.

Where to stay: Emerald Downs has special rates at several neighboring hotels. The best include the **Courtyard by Marriott** (253-529-0200) and the **Comfort Inn Auburn** (253-333-8888).

Where to eat: Right down the main drag from Emerald Downs is **BB Magraws Restaurant and Sports Bar** (440 16th St. NE; 253-804-5588). For a Mexican fiesta and a lively bar scene filled with racetrackers, head to **Las Margaritas** (1525 A St. NE; 253-735-9336).

Contact info: Call (253) 288-7000 for information, or call (888) 931-8400 to register. Entries are reserved on a first-come, first-served basis.

FAIR GROUNDS HANDICAPPING CONTEST

Where: Fair Grounds, New Orleans, Louisiana
When: December
Who: 150-200 entries (up to two entries per person)
How much: Entry fee of $200 includes an $80 real-money bankroll
Purse: $15,000 guaranteed
Scoreboard? No
DRF/NTRA qualifying spots: 3

Contest Rating: 4
Value Rating: 3
Qualifier Rating: 3 (Ratio – 50:1)

■

The Fair Grounds Handicapping Contest is held each December, providing horseplayers one of the final chances of the year to qualify for the National Handicapping Championship. Three DRF/NTRA qualifying spots are available in this contest. Fair Grounds' fourth and final qualifying spot to the national finals goes to the winner of a summer contest at the Finish Line OTB's in Louisiana.

Fair Grounds charges $200 to play in this contest, and that money is broken down into a $120 entry fee and an $80 real-money bankroll, which players use to bet with throughout the two-day contest. The track also offers a $25 rebate for people who enter the contest in advance. This lowers the cost to play in the contest to $95, plus your $80 live bankroll. Of course, all players get to keep all earnings compiled during the contest. Fair Grounds guarantees a $15,000 purse for the event, but promises to raise that amount if it receives more than a sufficient number of entries. The winner takes home first prize of $10,000, and payoffs are made down to fifth place.

This contest features a simple $2 win and $2 place format on a total of 10 races per day on both days of the two-day event. Wagers are divided into five mandatory plays and five optional plays per day on the live Fair Grounds races plus two simulcast tracks. There is no scoreboard, nor are there score updates provided in this contest, and there is no odds cap.

Why attend? This contest is one of the last chances to qualify for the national championship. The contest offers a lot of value, with the track returning nearly all entry fees in the form of prize money. Sign up in advance and save even more money ($25). The format features real-money bankrolls, so win or lose you still get to keep any earnings you compile during the contest.

Why not? No odds cap can be a big negative in a contest like this. There's nothing worse than leading a tournament all the way only to get nailed at the end by a player who blindly bets a 50-1 shot and wins.

How to win: The format of this contest is very good despite the fact that there is no odds cap. Normally, tournaments with no cap are longshot-stabbing contests, but that is not the case at Fair Grounds, because all bets are in real money and there is no scoreboard. Past Fair Grounds contests have been won with totals ranging from $174 to $146 based on $2 win-and-place bets on 20 races. Therefore, go ahead and buy two entries and aim for a final total over $150 in order to win and/or qualify.

Where to stay: Several area hotels offer special discounts when you ask for the Fair Grounds rates. Try the **Avenue Plaza Hotel** on St. Charles Ave. (504-566-1212) or the **Monteleone Hotel** on Royal St. (504-523-3341).

Where to eat: There are so many great restaurants in the area, and unfortunately it's impossible to list them all. You can't pass up on the world's greatest Cajun and Creole food when in New Orleans, so head on over to **Alex Patout's Louisiana Restaurant** (221 Royal St.; 504-525-7788), or **Mike Anderson's Seafood Restaurant** (215 Bourbon St.; 504-524-3884). **Crazy Johnnie's Café and Bar** (3520 18th St.; 504-887-6641) is also a racetrack favorite.

Contact info: Call 504-944-5515 for more information.

FAIR MEADOWS HANDICAPPING CONTEST

Where: Fair Meadows, Tulsa, Oklahoma
When: June, August, and October
Who: Each contest limited to 200
How much: Free to enter
Purse: $500
Scoreboard? No in preliminaries, yes in final round
DRF/NTRA qualifying spots: 4 total among 3 contests

Contest Rating:	3
Value Rating:	Free
Qualifier Rating:	2 (Ratio – 100:1)

■

Fair Meadows in Tulsa hosts three free one-day preliminary contests during the year to determine 21 finalists who will be invited back to the track at the end of the year to play for four available DRF/NTRA National Handicapping Championship qualifying spots and a top prize of $150. Seven qualifiers (plus ties) advance from each of the preliminaries. The first two preliminaries are based on $2 win and $2 place wagers on a total of 10 races including live races and simulcasts. In the third preliminary, Fair Meadows shakes things up a bit with an exacta contest where players are allowed a three-horse exacta box in each simulcast race they elect to play.

The final round will consist of $2 win and $2 place bets in a format similar to the National Handicapping Championship, with half the plays mandatory, and half optional. The top four finishers in the final round advance to Las Vegas and split $500 in prize money.

Why attend? If you've been sitting around waiting for an exacta contest to come along, your wishes have been answered. Call Fair Meadows for details on exactly when their next exacta contest will take place. Just like Fair Meadows' other handicapping contests, the exacta contest is free.

Why not? Even if you play well enough to win one of Fair Meadows' handicapping contests, you still won't necessarily qualify for the National Handicapping Championship. The three Fair Meadows handicapping contests only serve as preliminary events, so a win over 150 or so people is only enough to get you into their final round. Once there, you still need to finish in the top four out of a field of 21 in order to qualify for Las Vegas.

How to win: A couple of longshot plays are necessary to win this contest. In the past, a final bankroll in the neighborhood of $150 to $160 has been enough to place first in the Fair Meadows contests involving straight betting. Anything goes in Fair Meadows' exacta contest involving three-horse boxes, but it's logical to think you'd need to hit some high-priced combinations in order to win.

Where to stay: The perfect place to stay when visiting Fair Meadows is the **Microtel Tulsa Expo Center** (918-858-3775), which is located next to the track on the Tulsa Fair Grounds.

Where to eat: For steaks, seafood, pasta, Cajun food, and live music, there's no place near the track that's better than the **Bourbon Street Café** (1542 E. 15th St.; 918-583-5555). If you're looking for a neighborhood sports tavern, try **T-Town Sports Lounge** (725 N. Sheridan; 918-835-2325) or the **Varsity Sports Grill** (5840 S. Memorial Dr.; 918-622-5777).

Contact info: Call Fair Meadows at 918-746-3613.

FAIRPLEX PARK ROAD TO THE HANDICAPPER OF THE YEAR TOURNAMENT

Where: Fairplex Park, Pomona, California
When: September live meet
Who: Anyone at the track for any of the meet's first 16 days
How much: $100 entry fee, which serves as a player's betting stake
Purse: $800
Scoreboard? Yes
DRF/NTRA qualifying spots: 4

Contest Rating: 3
Value Rating: 3
Qualifier Rating: 5 (Ratio – 25:1)

■

Fairplex Park hosts a handicapping contest every day during its 17-day live Thoroughbred meet. The first 16 days are preliminary rounds and lead to the final round held on the last day of the meet. In order to advance to the final, players must either win one of the daily preliminary contests or compile one of the top 84 point totals during the length of the contest. Under this system, anywhere from 84 to 100 players could qualify for Fairplex's final round. Contestants may play all 16 days of the preliminary rounds, but every day is a different contest and points cannot be accumulated by a contestant who plays two or more days. Entrants can qualify for the final round only once. The top four scorers in the final round will all qualify for the National Handicapping Championship and each earn a $200 cash prize.

The tournament's betting format involves real-money wagering on any type of bet offered on the live race card at Fairplex Park, including exotic wagers. Players who wish to enter simply register for the contest and purchase a $100 account-wagering card for each day they wish to participate. Contestants must then try to build the highest possible bankroll by betting at least five races and $100 on the Fairplex races. Earnings can be re-bet throughout the day, and there is no maximum on how much you can play. Rules are the same in the final round as they are in the preliminaries, but the final is open only to players who have qualified.

Why attend? This contest is easy to enter. Just buy a contest card for
   $100 on any day of the meet and play exactly as you would on any day
   you go to the racetrack. The contest card works like a cash voucher, and

you keep the amount of money you have left on the card at the end of the day.

Why not? If you're coming from out of town, you will need to attend this contest a minimum of two separate days in order to advance to the national championship. First you'll need to play, and play well, in a preliminary round, and then you'll need to return to the track on the last day of the meet for the final, where you'll be up against between 83 and 99 rivals.

How to win: The name of the game is advancing to Fairplex's final round, so come to the track and play every day if necessary until you register a high enough score. Fairplex posts the scores of their previous days' winners as well as constantly updated listings of the top scorers, so you'll always know what amount you'll need to make it to the final round.

It's difficult to build up enough money by scattering your bets around in small increments throughout the day. Instead, try to make a couple big win bets and/or exacta bets during the day. Since the contest requires you to play at least five races, place nominal win, place, or show bets on a few races while saving enough of your money to unload on your two or three best bets of the day. You are allowed to re-bet your earnings, so take advantage of the rules by parlaying some of your early winnings on later races.

Tournament veteran Mike Labriola won this contest in 2000 with a final-round bankroll of $2,050. There can be a wide variation in scores, however, even within a single contest. In the contest won by Labriola with $2,050, the fourth-place finisher totaled only $675, which was also good enough to qualify for the national finals.

Where to stay: The best choice in the area is the **Sheraton Suites Fairplex** (909-622-2220). For the budget conscious, there's also a **Motel 6** (909-591-1871) in the area.

Where to eat: Just outside the racetrack on the grounds of the **Los Angeles County Fair** there are a hundred food stands serving just about everything you could want. Check the fair schedule for the dates of the beer and wine competitions.

Contact info: Call Fairplex at 909-865-4093.

GOLDEN GATE/DRF HANDICAPPING CHALLENGE

Where: Golden Gate Fields, Albany/Berkeley, California
When: November-December
Who: 4,000 entries expected
How much: Free
Purse: $5,000
Scoreboard? No
DRF/NTRA qualifying spots: 4

Contest Rating: 2
Value Rating: Free
Qualifier Rating: 1 (Ratio – 250:1)

■

Golden Gate puts its four DRF/NTRA National Handicapping Championship qualifying spots up for grabs in a free contest spanning the final two months of the year. The contest consists of two preliminary rounds and a final round. Round One takes place over a three- or four-day period. Contestants pick up entry blanks and attempt to select at least one show horse on any given first-round day. Participants may play more than one day if necessary, but can only earn one second-round entry per person. Successful handicappers (almost everyone) will then receive a letter inviting them to play in the Golden Gate second round four weeks later. For the second round, advancing players must select at least one place horse on the day's live race card. Players who are successful in Round Two (again, almost everyone) can then advance to the Bay Meadows final round. Second-round players can earn only one final-round berth per person. In the final, qualifying players must try to select the winners of Bay Meadows races 3 through 8. The players in the final round who amass the highest totals based on mythical $2 wagers will qualify for the National Handicapping Championship and split $5,000 in prize money.

Note: The 2002 DRF/NTRA Handicapper of the Year, Herman Miller, qualified for the National Handicapping Championship with a fourth-place finish in this event on December 29, 2001, making him the final qualifier in the final qualifying contest for that year's national finals.

Why attend? This is a free contest offering $5,000 in prize money and four qualifying spots in the National Handicapping Championship.
Why not? This contest requires three separate trips to Golden Gate,

and odds of earning a berth in Las Vegas are still small since thousands of people will enter.

How to win: You must show up at the track for every round. This may seem simple, but just the process of coming to the track three separate times is likely to thin the field down to about 1,000 local finalists. With so many players competing in the finals, you'll probably need to go at least 5 for 6 or maybe even 6 for 6 in order to have a chance to win.

Where to stay: The **Radisson Hotel Berkeley Marina** (510-548-7920) is just one exit down from the racetrack on Highway 80 west toward the bay. There's also a **Holiday Inn Express** (510-548-1700) nearby in Berkeley.

Where to eat: A good place for some beer and grub after the races is **Pyramid Alehouse** (901 Gilman St.; 510-528-9880), located just six blocks from Golden Gate Fields. **Skates on the Bay** (100 Seawall Dr.; 510-549-1900) is one exit down the highway located right on the water. Another racetrack hangout is **Little Ange's** (6115 Potrero Ave.; 510-232-8979), which is known for its good, low-priced menu. **Little Ange's** is especially popular with the track crowd every Thursday.

Contact info: Call Golden Gate at 510-559-7300 or dial 650-573-4617.

GULFSTREAM PARK'S TURF-VIVOR HANDICAPPING CONTEST
*Recommended

Where: Gulfstream Park, Hallandale, Florida
When: February
Who: Maximum of 125 entries
Purse: Guaranteed purse of $132,000-$140,000
How much: $1,000 entry fee
Scoreboard: Only in final round
DRF/NTRA qualifying spots: 4

Contest Rating: 3
Value Rating 4
Qualifier Rating: 4 (Ratio – 31:1)

■

If you are tired of the same old tournament formats in contest after contest, you might want to consider playing in Gulfstream's Turf-vivor handicapping contest. Turf-vivor features two days of across-the-board betting and a final-round tournament-bracket format that pairs up the top 16 players in head-to-head combat to determine Gulfstream's four National Handicapping Championship qualifiers.

The inaugural Turf-vivor contest in 2002 drew a positive response from its 120 entrants, and will return in February 2003 with an even better format featuring between $132,000 and $140,000 in guaranteed prize money. The entry fee has been raised from $750 to $1,000, but the size of the field is now limited to 125 entries as opposed to 225 in 2002.

For the first two days of the three-day contest, players must build the highest possible bankroll in a total of 10 mandatory races (five per day) with $2 across-the-board wagers on a single horse per race. Odds are capped at 20-1 to win, 10-1 to place, and 5-1 to show. The 16 highest-scoring players will then advance to the final round, where they will go head-to-head in a tournament-bracket-style format with the No. 1 seeded player playing No. 16, and so on. Head-to-head contests will be won by the player who collects the most money in a two-race playoff. In the event of a tie, the higher-seeded player advances. The process repeats itself as the field is paired down to the elite eight, the final four, and then to the one ultimate "Turf-vivor."

The winner of the contest earns a $100,000 first prize, with $10,000 going to the runner-up and $2,500 each going to third and fourth. The final four all qualify for Las Vegas. Every player who makes it to Turf-vivor's sweet 16 earns $500, and additional daily prizes will also be offered to raise the purse to between $132,000 and $140,000.

Why attend? This contest format is imaginative and offers a change of pace for those who are sick of the same old, same old. The winner gets a big check for $100,000, and odds of qualifying for the DRF/NTRA finals aren't bad with four spots available to the field of 125 players.

Why not? The whole idea of this contest is to finish in the top 16 and advance into the tournament brackets on the final day (Sunday). If you miss the cut, however, you go home after only two days and cannot play on Sunday. Every one of the top 16 finishers is guaranteed at least half the entry fee back ($500), but the contest is still rather top heavy, with the first four finishers taking home the majority of the money.

How to win: Normal tournament rules apply throughout the first two days of the contest. You'll need winners and plenty of them to build a high enough bankroll to reach the sweet 16. All participants must play the same races, so if a 20-1 horse wins and you don't have it, you may be done. In the final-round tournament brackets, the huge advantage goes to the higher-seeded player. Players go head-to-head for two races and the higher seed always wins the tie-breaker—including $0 - $0 ties. Higher seeds must play defensively, betting horses that can hurt them. The most important thing for lower seeds is to try to pick winners and try to put some money in the bank without worrying too much about the odds.

Where to stay: Budget-minded players can get a lot of bang for their buck at the nearby **Holiday Inn Express** (954-456-8333), which is just 10 minutes away from the track down Hallandale Beach Blvd. at the junction of I-95. **The Holiday Inn Sunspree Resort** (954-923-9700), a moderately priced place on the beach in Hollywood, is a favorite of horsemen and may offer reduced rates for tournament players. Those who want to stay closer to the action of South Beach may want to consider the high-end **Sheraton Bal Harbor Resort** (305-865-7511) just 20 minutes south of the track.

Where to eat: For good steaks and a lively bar right down the street from the track head to **Manero's** (2600 E. Hallandale Beach Blvd.; 954-456-1000). **Chef Allen's** in North Miami Beach offers fine French and continental dining (19088 N.E. 29th Ave.; 305-935-2900). No visit to the Miami area would be complete without a trip to **Joe's Stone Crab** in South Beach (227 Biscayne St., 305-673-0365), but be prepared to wait hours for a table.

Contact info: Call (954) 457-6185 or (954) 847-6187, or visit *www.gulfstreampark.com.*

HAWTHORNE/SPORTSMAN'S HANDICAPPING CONTEST

Where: Hawthorne Race Course (Chicago area)
When: April
Who: No limit to how many can enter. The contest is free, so expect between 600 and 700 entries at each of the two qualifying rounds.
How much: Free
Purse: Total prize money is $4,800
Scoreboard? Yes, in final round
DRF/NTRA qualifying spots: 4

Contest Rating: 3
Value Rating: Free
Qualifier Rating: 1 (Ratio – 300:1)

Sportsman's Park, which now runs its National Jockey Club meet literally across the street at Hawthorne, holds two preliminary rounds on consecutive Saturdays, and then a final round the following Saturday. In the preliminaries, players simply pick up entry forms, and hand them in with their win selections on six predetermined on-track races. The top 50 finishers on each preliminary Saturday, based on the number of winning selections, can advance to the final round.

Out of the 100 preliminary qualifiers (50 from each day), roughly 70 or 80 can typically be expected back for the Sportsman's at Hawthorne final round. Therefore, with four National Handicapping Championship spots on the table, final-round participants have about a 1 in 20 chance at qualifying for Las Vegas.

In the final round, a similar format is used except with the added dimension of mutuel payoffs. Finalists must pick one horse in six preselected races from Hawthorne, and the players who earn the highest bankrolls based on $2 win and $2 place bets will win.

The top four finishers win $1,000 in addition to trips to Las Vegas for the National Handicapping Championship. The eight next-highest finishers receive $100 prizes.

Why attend? The contest is free to enter, so anyone at the track on the days of the event won't even need to go out of his or her way in order to participate. The contest is uncomplicated. Just pick winners in order to qualify for Sportsman's final round. The track is putting up prize money and four qualifying spots, and it costs the players nothing.

Why not? The odds are stacked against you. In order to win money and qualify for the National Handicapping Championship, you'll have to finish in the top 100 out of a field of 600 to 700 people in the preliminary rounds, and then finish in the top four out of 70 to 100 people in the final round. The contest also lacks tournament atmosphere. All players do is select horses, fill out their entry forms, and then wait and see the results. Not much of a competitive atmosphere, but at least the price is right.

How to win: Since mutuel prices are not a factor until the final round, try your best to pick as many winners as possible in the preliminaries, regardless of odds. This is one of the rare cases in handicapping contests where it is actually in your best interest to pick favorites and low-priced horses. If you don't advance to the final round on the first qualifying Saturday, you are welcome to come back and try again the next Saturday.

Once you've made it to the finals, use traditional tournament strategy to grow your bankroll. Since everyone in the contest must play the same six races, you don't only want to bet longshots because a single winner paying $6.80 could end up making a difference. Bet logical horses and mix in horses in the 5-1 to 10-1 range because it's tough to win a contest like this unless you hit the highest-priced horse in the six-race sequence.

The winner of Sportsman's 2002 contest totaled $33.60, but that contest included only $2 win wagering and no place wagering. The fourth-place finisher had $28.40. Therefore, with place betting thrown into the mix this year, try to set a goal of a final bankroll in the $40 to $50 range for the six races.

Where to stay: If you have a car, stay downtown at the **Westin Chicago River North** (312-744-1900) so you can be within walking distance of Chicago's great attractions, including the Magnificent Mile. Budget-minded fans who want to stay close to the track can try the **Sportsman's Inn Motel** (773-582-3700), just a few blocks away on Cicero Avenue.

Where to eat: Sportsman's Park is in an industrial area just west of Chicago, and there's no reason to eat anywhere nearby except at the racetrack. Instead, take a ride downtown and try **Harry Caray's Restaurant** (33 W. Kinzie St.; 212-828-0966). For great, upscale Oaxacan Mexican food, go to the **Frontera Grill** and **Tompolobampo** (445 N. Clark St.; 212-661-1434).

Contact info: Call 773-242-1121 and ask for tournament coordinator Scott McMannis.

KING OF HOLLYWOOD PARK HANDICAPPING CONTEST   *Recommended

Where: Hollywood Park, Inglewood, California
When: November-December
Who: Estimated 5,000 entries
How much: Free
Purse: $75,000
Scoreboard? No
DRF/NTRA qualifying spots: 4

Contest Rating: 4
Value Rating: Free
Qualifier Rating: 1 (Ratio – 1,250:1)

■

Hollywood Park hosts a free daily handicapping contest on six days throughout its fall meet, with $75,000 in daily prizes over the duration of the event.

Players may bet a mythical $100 a day on races 5 through 9 only at Hollywood Park, with no more than $20 wagered per race. Win, place, show, exacta, quinella, trifecta, and superfecta wagers are accepted as long as the total bet per race does not exceed $20. Winnings cannot be re-wagered, and money not wagered will not count toward a player's total. The top nine overall finishers will split $45,000 in prize money with $20,000 going to the cumulative winner. The contest also features $30,000 in daily prizes, with $5,000 going to each daily winner and additional cash prizes down to fifth place each day. Either the top four overall contest winners or the four top finishers from a single preselected contest day will earn Hollywood Park's four spots to the DRF/NTRA National Handicapping Championship.

Why attend? The contest costs nothing, but Hollywood Park puts up serious prize money of $75,000 and four trips to the National Handicapping Championship.

Why not? While this contest does offer value, there is no real contest atmosphere, with entry blanks taking the place of a proper tournament.

How to win: If you can play every day, you can build up a good enough bankroll just by doing well with straight bets and maybe the occasional exacta. If you can only enter on a couple different days, go for the daily prize money or else plop all your money into ridiculous trifectas and superfectas and hope for lightning to strike. If you hit a $10,000 superfecta, maybe your aggregate one- or two-day total will be enough to win the whole enchilada. If the National Handicapping Championship qualifying spots go to the winners of a single daily contest instead of the aggregate winners, make sure you at least show up once for that day's contest.

Where to stay: The **Crown Plaza Los Angeles-Intl. Airport** (310-642-7500) is the official hotel of Hollywood Park. Mention the special Hollywood Park rate or corporate ID #100858473.

Where to eat: There's not a lot happening in the area around Hollywood Park after the races, but the **Houston's** in Manhattan Beach (1550 A Rosecrans Ave.; 310-463-7211) is a popular stop after the races. **The Cheesecake Factory** in Marina Del Rey (4142 Via Marina; 310-306-3344) has a terrific location overlooking the ocean.

Contact info: Call Hollywood Park at 310-419-1500 and follow the prompts to connect to the marketing department.

HOOSIER PARK QUALIFYING TOURNAMENT   *Recommended

Where: Hoosier Park, Anderson, Indiana
When: November
Who: No limit to entries, but a little more than 100 are expected
How much: $100 entry fee
Purse: $6,750
Scoreboard? Yes, updates every half-hour
DRF/NTRA qualifying spots: 4

Contest Rating: 4
Value Rating: 3
Qualifier Rating: 5 (Ratio – 25:1)

■

Hoosier Park in central Indiana hosts a one-day contest during its live fall Thoroughbred meet. This is an excellent place to go to qualify for the National Handicapping Championship, because the field size is relatively small (about 100 entries are expected), and all four DRF/NTRA qualifying spots are available in a single, one-day event. Multiple entries per person are also accepted. The entry fee is $100, which includes parking, admission, program, lunch, and a Hoosier Park T-shirt and goody bag. The contest guarantees $6,750 in purse money including $5,000 to the winner, $1,000 for second, $500 for third, and $250 for fourth.

Players will place a total of 40 wagers in the tournament. Each participant must make $2 to win and $2 to place wagers on 20 selected races. All races will be chosen by tournament organizers and are likely to include races from Aqueduct, Calder, Churchill Downs, and Hollywood Park. Hoosier is running its live meet at the time of its contest, but live racing is at night and the tournament is during the day. Therefore, there will be no betting on Hoosier Park's live races for contest purposes. Winners will be determined by the total combined mutuel payoffs of all winning selections. Odds are capped at 20-1 ($42) to win and 10-1 ($22) to place.

Why attend? If you are traveling around from contest to contest in order to qualify for the National Handicapping Championship, this is one of the most qualifier-friendly spots on the tournament calendar. All four national-finals spots will be decided on one day, and the races involved in the betting are all well-known simulcast signals. There's no local racing involved in the tournament.

Why not? There could be a very big takeout in this contest based on a large field. Once the amount of entries goes higher than 67, you'll be facing a higher and higher takeout for every additional entrant in the contest. In other words, a small amount of entries benefits the players and a large amount of entries benefits the track.

How to win: This is a new contest format for Hoosier Park, so there's not a lot of past information to help you. Find out what the top four scores were in the November 2002 contest, and proceed from there. Count on needing to at least double your original $80 bankroll. In order to do so, you'll need some high-priced winners. Take advantage of the rule allowing multiple entries per person, and purchase as many entries as they'll allow (or as many as you can afford).

Where to stay: Hoosier Park is affiliated with two nearby hotels including **Comfort Inn** (765-649-3000) and **Hampton Inn Anderson** (765-622-0707). The **Hampton Inn** features free continental breakfast and free local calls.

Where to eat: A good spot in Anderson before or after the races is **Applebee's** (1922 E. 53rd St.; 765-642-7763). **Gene's Root Beer Stand** (640 S. Scatterfield Rd.; 765-642-5768) is a local landmark as well as the oldest drive-in restaurant in the state of Indiana.

Contact info: Call Hoosier Park at 800-526-7223 and try extensions 1033 or 1044 for details.

HORSEMEN'S PARK DRF/NTRA QUALIFYING CONTEST

Where: Horsemen's Park, Omaha, Nebraska
When: Four contests: May, August, and October (2)
Who: 400 to 500 entrants per contest
How much: Free to enter
Purse: $1,000 for each contest
Scoreboard? Yes, constant updates
DRF/NTRA qualifying spots: 4 total spots, 1 per contest

Contest Rating:	3
Value Rating:	Free
Qualifier Rating:	1 (Ratio – 450:1)

■

Horsemen's Park in Omaha hosts four extremely popular handicapping contests a year, each with one available qualifying spot to the National Handicapping Championship. Steven Walker, the first DRF/NTRA Handicapper of the Year winner, qualified for the national finals at this contest in 1999. The Horsemen's Park contests normally attract 400 to 500 entrants (one entry per person) to the track's huge simulcast facility that features 675 television screens and simulcast racing from around the country. All contests are free to enter, but the track kicks in $1,000 in prizes for each of the four events, with $200 going to the winner, and payoffs no smaller than $50 going to the top 10 finishers.

Three of the four contests have the same format, with players picking all races at two simulcast tracks (normally one each from New York and Southern California). Contestants receive five points for every winner, and two points for every pick that finishes second. Players also select a best bet at each of the two contest tracks. Winning best bets are worth five bonus points. Mutuel prices are not considered except in the event of ties, in which case total combined mutuel prices serve as the tie-breaker. The first of the four annual contests at Horsemen's Park involves a series of Saturday contests revolving around spring races. The top weekly finishers advance to Horsemen's Park's Spring Champions Contest, which offers a trip to the National Handicapping Championship to its winner.

Why attend? Every one of these contests offers a free shot at a trip to the National Handicapping Championship as well as a $1,000 purse that the track throws in as a bonus.

Why not? The odds of winning this contest are very slim, with 400 to

500 people competing for just one DRF/NTRA qualifying spot per contest. Oh, well . . . as lottery players like to say, "somebody's gonna win."

How to win: You must try to pick a winner in every race at two tracks, meaning that each contest consists of roughly 20 races. Don't worry about mutuel prices. Concentrate on picking winners because you're most likely going to need more than 10 winners to have a shot.

Where to stay: There are several hotels close to Horsemen's Park, including **Holiday Inn-Omaha** (402-393-3950) and **Howard Johnson's** (402-339-7400).

Where to eat: The **Winchester Saloon Bar & Grill** (7002 Q. St.; 402-331-9333) has good pub grub and is the closest restaurant/watering hole to the track. There are also five sand volleyball courts and karaoke on Wednesdays and Thursdays.

Contact info: Call Horsemen's Park at 402-734-8464.

KEENELAND HANDICAPPING CHALLENGE

Where: Keeneland, Lexington, Kentucky
When: August and December
Who: Limited to 500
How much: $100 entry fee (maximum three entries per person)
Purse: $19,250 for each contest
Scoreboard? Yes, race-by-race computer printouts
DRF/NTRA qualifying spots: 8 (four in each of two contests)

Contest Rating:	4
Value Rating:	2
Qualifier Rating:	2 (Ratio – 100:1)

■

Keeneland hosts two Handicapping Challenges per year, one in the summer and one in the fall following Keeneland's live fall race meet. Instead of splitting up one set of four DRF/NTRA qualifying spots between the two contests, Keeneland has gone the extra mile by sending two separate teams of four qualifiers (Keeneland "A" and Keeneland "B") to the national finals. Note: The Keeneland "A" team from its August 2001 contest won the team competition in National Handicapping Championship III in January 2002.

Keeneland's contests are one-day events consisting of 12 total races.

Keeneland is dark during both contests, so simulcast races from a wide variety of locations are offered, including New York, Southern California, Kentucky, and Chicago tracks plus Calder and River Downs. Half of the 12 races are mandatory, and the other half are optional plays at any of the tracks offered for betting. The winners are the entrants who accumulate the highest earnings based on the 12 mythical $2-to-win, $2-to-place wagers available. All payoffs are capped at 20-1 to win ($42) and 10-1 ($22) to place. Each contest costs $100 to enter and is open to as many as 500 entries. Both contests offer prize money of $19,250, with $10,000 going to the winner and lesser cash payoffs down to 20th place.

Why attend? Keeneland's contests are set up with a format similar to the one used in the National Handicapping Championship, and there is a large amount of good simulcast racing on the wagering menu. The contests cost only $100 to enter and multiple entries per person are allowed (three maximum).

Why not? These contests have potentially very large takeouts if field size reaches anywhere near the limit of 500. Technically, a field size any larger than 192 entries means Keeneland won't be returning 100 percent of all entry fees in the form of prize money. Based on a full field, or anything close to it, the contest's takeout will be more than 50 percent, and that's not good. Also, while the first prize of $10,000 is good, there is a sharp drop-off from there, with $3,000 going to second, and only $1,500, $1,200, and $800 going to the third- through fifth-place finishers.

How to win: First make sure to buy three entries. The $100 entry fee is very reasonable, and you've got to take advantage of three entries when they are offered. Besides, if you're playing in this contest, you probably already know that the takeout is ridiculous and what you're really here for are the four DRF/NTRA qualifying spots. You have a wide selection of optional races in this contest, so pick out mid- to long-priced horses you really like in those six races and try to hit a home run. Bet sensibly in the mandatory races, but realize that you probably need to hit the highest-priced winner in those six required events if you want to have a chance to win. A recent winner of this contest scored $219.50 in earnings (in 12 races!), but a more reasonable total of $149.90 was enough to finish in the top four and qualify for the National Handicapping Championship.

Where to stay: One of the best-known hotels in Lexington is **The**

Springs Inn (859-277-5751), a reasonably priced place that is often filled with racing fans and horsemen. Another good choice within easy driving distance of Keeneland is the **Campbell House Inn, Suites and Golf Club** (859-255-4281). Also recommended is the **Gratz Park Inn** (859-231-1777), a historic downtown inn that is home to Jonathan's, one of Lexington's finest restaurants.

Where to eat: A new Lexington hot spot that attracts young racegoers as well as the local racing establishment is **Emmett's** (Tates Creek Rd. and Duval Dr.; 859-254-4444), which features a formal dining area as well as a bar with a fireplace. **Dudley's** (380 S. Mill St.; 859-252-1010) is a good restaurant and bar with a horsy atmosphere and clientele. **Malone's** (located in the Lansdowne Shoppes on Tates Creek Rd.; 859-335-6500) is a steakhouse that draws many local trainers and owners.

Contact info: Call 859-288-4261 for more information.

LAUREL'S MJC CHAMPIONS TOURNAMENT

Where: Laurel
When: Laurel's fall meet
Who: Field size limited to 250
How much: Entry fee of $100 plus a $200 real-money bankroll
Purse: $10,000 guaranteed
Scoreboard? No
DRF/NTRA qualifying spots: 2

Contest Rating:	2
Value Rating:	4
Qualifier Rating:	3 (Ratio – 50:1)

■

Laurel's MJC Champions Tournament is the second of two contests held each year by Maryland Jockey Club tracks. The top two finishers from Laurel's contest join the top two finishers at Pimlico to comprise the Maryland Jockey Club's four-person team at the National Handicapping Championship finals.

The Laurel format is the same as the Pimlico format. The one-day contest features a live, real-money bankroll of $200. The idea in the contest, just as in a typical day at the races, is to accumulate the highest possible bankroll by the end of the proceedings. This contest uses a wide-open format that allows almost all different kinds of bets on both on-track races and simulcast races. There is no minimum or maximum amount to bet, and no minimum or maximum number of races to play.

All betting in this contest is parimutuel, and any bet, including win, place, show, and exotics, is permitted in the contest, with the exception of multi-race bets (such as pick threes, pick fours, etc.) at simulcast tracks. This rule is in place strictly to increase mutuel churn and prevent too much contest money from getting tied up for long periods of time on out-of-state-races.

The size of the field is not limited, but always ends up in the 90 to 110 range. Entry fee is $100 (plus your $200 bankroll), and prize money is guaranteed at $10,000 regardless of how many people enter.

Why attend? With a guaranteed purse of $10,000, this contest offers entrants a good value if fewer than 100 people enter (100 x $100 = $10,000). For example, with 95 players, Pimlico will be taking in only $9,500 but still paying $10,000 in prize money. The track gives players the value-added perk of $20 in Players' Choice Bucks, which can be spent like real money anywhere at the track, including restaurants and concessions stands.

Why not? If more than 100 players enter, the contest loses its value because the track still only pays out $10,000 in prize money. For example, if 110 people enter at $100 each, the track will collect $11,000 but only pay back $10,000. With a wide-open format involving no minimum or maximum amount of bets, and the option of making almost any kind of wager at any track, this contest lacks a competitive tournament environment and atmosphere. The fact that there is no designated tournament room or area also takes away from the fun.

How to win: Chipping away with win, place, or show bets may not do you much good here if others are playing, and winning, bets like pick fours and superfectas. You probably won't be able to win this event by treating it like a normal day at the track, even if you happen to be having a good day.

Since there is no minimum on how many bets you make, this type of contest is usually won by the player or players who hit big with a pick three, trifecta, or superfecta, and then stand pat on top of their mountain of earnings. The other winning strategy is to take your entire $200 bankroll and bet it all to win on your single best bet of the day. If your horse wins and pays just 5-1, you could be sitting pretty with a total of over $1,200 from your original $200 bankroll. Even if you come up short, you'll still be taking home a profit of $1,000 in this scenario, which isn't too shabby.

Take a look at both winning strategies and pick which one works best for you. If you're the type of person who doesn't mind losing $200 on a single bet, you might want to roll the dice and bet it all to win on one horse. If you want to give yourself a chance to win without risking your whole $200, play a couple big exotics part-wheels and hope you can parlay a well-timed score into a trip to Las Vegas.

Where to stay: There's a **Red Roof Inn** (301-498-8811) right down the street from the track. Another motel in the area is the **Econo Lodge Laurel Racetrack** (301-776-8008).

Where to eat: You can't go to Maryland and not try the fresh seafood, so head on over to the **Bay-N-Surf Seafood Restaurant** (14411 Baltimore Ave.; 301-776-7021). For steaks, go to **Sullivan's Steak & Beverage** (9624 Fort Meade Rd.; 301-498-7427).

Contact info: Call 301-725-0400 and ask for information on Laurel's next contest.

LONE STAR PARK DRF/NTRA HANDICAPPER OF THE YEAR QUALIFYING TOURNAMENT

Where: Lone Star Park, Grand Prairie, Texas
When: June
Who: Roughly 100 players (no limit)
How much: Base entry is $100, but Star Players members pay only $50. Late entries cost $200.
Purse: Cash prizes of $1,850
Scoreboard? Yes, but only on Day Two
DRF/NTRA qualifying spots: 4

Contest Rating:	3
Value Rating:	1
Qualifier Rating:	5 (Ratio – 25:1)

■

The format of this two-day contest is nearly identical to that of the National Handicapping Championship. Players make mythical $2 win and $2 place bets (same horse) on 20 races a day on both days of the contest for a total of 40 races. Just as in the National Handicapping Championship, daily plays will include 10 mandatory races and 10 others to be chosen by the players from several different tournament tracks. Most recently, Lone Star used races from four tracks—Arlington,

Belmont, Churchill, and Lone Star—in its contest, with a wide assortment of stakes and feature races chosen as the mandatory events.

This contest has been around for a number of years, but it has never really been a big success. Lone Star seems to put much more energy into some other promotions, such as the All-Star Jockey Championship. There is no maximum number of players allowed in this contest, but roughly 100 can be expected to participate based on past showings (97 entered in 2002). The contest costs $100 to enter, but members of Lone Star Park's Star Player program get into the field at half price. Late entries (past the entry deadline) are accepted at $200 a pop. The contest offers prize money of $1,850 with $1,000 to the winner, $500 for second, $250 for third, and $100 for fourth. The top four finishers also qualify for the DRF/NTRA National Handicapping Championship.

Why attend? This contest has a good tournament format that closely approximates the format of the DRF/NTRA national finals in Las Vegas. The two-day event features both players'-choice and mandatory races, and there is good racing to choose from with live races and three simulcast tracks open for betting. This contest offers a great opportunity to qualify for the National Handicapping Championship with only about 100 entrants vying for four qualifying spots.

Why not? This contest offers a horrible return on investment, with only about 20 percent of all entry fees being returned to the winners in the form of prize money. That equates to something like an 80 percent takeout. The contest is also top heavy, with the first four finishers splitting all the cash in addition to the four trips to the National Handicapping Championship.

How to win: With four tracks to choose from, you'll have enough of a selection to play only the kinds of races you excel at, and you'll have access to at least one or two tracks you're highly familiar with. Pick your spots and wait for high-odds horses, overlays, and horses offering value in big fields. Play the mandatory races the same way, finding value in the big, wide-open races while plugging away with as many winners as you can hit in the short fields containing a few obvious contenders.

Where to stay: There are several hotel chains in Grand Prairie surrounding the track. Try the **Comfort Inn Grand Prairie** (866-597-9330), or the **Hampton Inn Arlington/DFW Airport** (866-597-9330).

Where to eat: The **Fox and Hound** (1001 NE Green Oaks Blvd.; 817-277-3591) is an English-style brew pub in Arlington that is a popular hangout for locals and racetrack folks alike. Also in Arlington, don't forget the Cajun Foodfest at **Pappadeaux's** (1304 Copeland Rd. at Collins; 817-543-0545), the home of the famous Swamp Thing and Authentic Hurricane drinks.

Contact info: Call (972) 237-1134 or (972) 283-RACE for more information.

LOS ALAMITOS HANDICAPPING CHALLENGE

Where: Los Alamitos Racecourse, Los Alamitos, California
When: Summer
Who: All on-track patrons welcome (400 entered in 2002)
How much: Free to enter
Purse: $2,000
Scoreboard? No
DRF/NTRA qualifying spots: 4

Contest Rating: 2
Value Rating: Free
Qualifier Rating: 2 (Ratio – 100:1)

■

The Los Alamitos Handicapping Challenge is a free, one-day contest open to anyone who shows up at the track on the day of the event (limit one entry per person). Participants get an entry blank and are asked to fill in the winners of six specific races including both on-track events and a couple simulcasts from Hollywood Park. The players who select the most winners, regardless of payoffs, are the winners. In the likely event of a tie for either first, second, third, or fourth place, mutuel payoffs for win, and then win and place, will determine the winners. Los Alamitos provides a purse of $2,000 with $900 going to the winner, $400 for second, $240 for third, and $100 for fourth. Everyone in the top 20 receives at least $20.

Why attend? The contest costs nothing to enter and Los Alamitos ponies up $2,000 of its own money for prizes, which is a good deal no matter how you slice it. The contest also gives fans a free shot at four qualifying spots to the DRF/NTRA National Handicapping Championship.

Why not? It's hard to find things wrong with a free contest, but the Los Alamitos Handicapping Challenge is as bare-bones as it gets. You turn in an entry blank and wait for the results—that's it. There isn't much strategy involved and the odds against you are 100-1 based on 400 entries.

How to win: Picking winners is the name of the game, but you can't completely ignore mutuel prices with ties likely to happen among the top finishers. Depending on how many upsets there are in the six races used in the contest, as many as five wins in six races could be necessary in order to finish in the top four. Count on needing at least four winners to qualify, and if four is all you have you're sure to be in a multi-way tie, so don't forget to pick at least a couple good prices.

Where to stay: The closest hotel to Los Alamitos Racecourse is the **Best Western Los Alamitos Inn and Suites** (562-598-2299), which is within a mile of the track on Los Alamitos Blvd.

Where to eat: If you can't muster the strength to head to Los Angeles or at least Anaheim, stay in Los Alamitos and enjoy the local flavor right across the street from the track at **The Starting Gate Saloon and Steakhouse** (5052 W. Katella Ave.; 562-598-8957). Sports fans can get some grub while checking out the latest scores at **Mr. B's Restaurant and Sports Lounge** (11272 Los Alamitos Blvd.; 562-430-0213).

Contact info: Call Los Alamitos at (714) 820-2690.

PIMLICO PLAYERS' CHOICE HANDICAPPING TOURNAMENT

Where: Pimlico
When: April
Who: Field size not limited, but 90 to 110 entries are the norm.
How much: Entry fee of $100 plus a $200 real-money bankroll
Purse: $10,000 guaranteed
Scoreboard? No
DRF/NTRA qualifying spots: 2

Contest Rating:	2
Value Rating:	5
Qualifier Rating:	3 (Ratio – 50:1)

■

The Pimlico Players' Choice Tournament is a one-day contest that features a live, real-money bankroll. Just like a typical day at the races, you keep whatever you win at the mutuel windows. The idea of the contest is to replicate an actual day at the track with a wide-open format that allows almost all different kinds of bets on both on-track races and simulcast events. There is no minimum or maximum amount to bet, and no minimum or maximum number of races to play. The only thing that counts is how much money you have in your bankroll at the end of the contest.

All betting in this contest is parimutuel, and any type of bet, including win, place, show, and exotics, is permitted in the contest, with the exception of multi-race bets (such as pick threes, pick fours, etc.) at simulcast tracks. This rule is in place strictly to increase mutuel churn and prevent too much contest money from getting tied up for long periods of time on out-of-state-races.

The size of the field is not limited, but always ends up in the 90 to 110 range. Entry fee is $100 (plus your $200 bankroll), and prize money is guaranteed at $10,000 regardless of how many people enter.

Why attend? With a guaranteed purse of $10,000, this contest offers entrants a great value if fewer than 100 people enter (100 x $100 = $10,000). For example, with 95 players, Pimlico will be taking in only $9,500 but still paying $10,000 in prize money. The track also gives players the value-added perk of $20 in Players' Choice Bucks, which can be spent like real money anywhere at the track including restaurants and concessions stands.

Why not? If more than 100 players enter, the contest loses its value because the track still only pays out $10,000 in prize money. For example, if 110 people enter at $100 each, the track will collect $11,000 but only pay back $10,000. With a wide-open format involving no minimum or maximum amount of bets, and the option of making almost any kind of wager at any track, this contest lacks a competitive tournament environment and atmosphere. The fact that there is no designated tournament room or area also takes away from the fun.

How to win: Chipping away with win, place, or show bets may not do you much good here if others are playing, and winning, bets like pick fours and superfectas. (The top two finishers in the 2002 contest won thanks to exotic bets with big payoffs.) You probably won't be able to win this event by treating it like a normal day at the track, even if you happen to be having a good day.

Since there is no minimum to how many bets you make, this type of contest is usually won by the player or players who hit a big pick three, trifecta, or superfecta, and then stand pat on top of their mountain of earnings. The other winning strategy is to take your entire $200 bankroll, and bet it all to win on your single best bet of the day. If your horse wins and pays just 5-1, you could be sitting pretty with a total of over $1,200 from your original $200 bankroll. Even if you come up short, you'll still be taking home a profit of $1,000 in this scenario, which isn't too shabby. Take a look at both winning strategies and pick which one works best for you. If you're the type of person who doesn't mind losing $200 on a single bet, you might want to roll the dice and bet it all to win on one horse. If you want to give yourself a chance to win without risking your whole $200, play a couple big exotics part-wheels and hope you can parlay a well-timed score into a trip to Las Vegas.

Where to stay: There's not much near the track except the **Baltimore-Days Inn East** (410-882-0900) which is about three miles away in neighboring Towson. If you're making a trip to Pimlico and to Baltimore in general, do yourself a favor and stay downtown near the Inner Harbor. You can't go wrong at the **Sheraton Inner Harbor** (410-962-8300) or at any one of the other national hotel chains in the area.

Where to eat: **Koopers Tavern** (1702 Thames St.; 410-563-5423) is one of many good restaurant/bars in the Fells Point neighborhood of Baltimore on the waterfront. Also in the same area is **Bo Brooks at Lighthouse Point** (410-558-0202), which is one of Baltimore's best crab houses.

Contact info: Call 410-578-4433 for more information.

PRAIRIE MEADOWS DRF/NTRA QUALIFYING TOURNAMENT
*Recommended

Where: Prairie Meadows, Altoona, Iowa
When: June and September
Who: Limited to 100, but 75 to 80 is normal
How much: Entry fee is $50
Purse: $5,000 based on 100 entries
Scoreboard? Yes, during the second half of the contest
DRF/NTRA qualifying spots: 2 in each contest

Contest Rating: 5 summer, 3 fall
Value Rating: 4
Qualifier Rating: 4 (Ratio – 40:1)

Prairie Meadows is well worth a visit for at least one of its two annual contests, which each offer two qualifying spots to the DRF/NTRA National Handicapping Championship. Prairie's first contest is held during its spring-summer Thoroughbred meet, with the second coming late in the mixed Thoroughbred/Quarter Horse meet that lasts till early fall. The contests feature small fields and entry fees of only $50, which makes them a good, inexpensive place to take a shot at qualifying for the big dance.

Both Prairie Meadows contests are one-day events featuring the full card from Prairie Meadows plus five or six preselected simulcast races from a variety of tracks. Players must make mythical $2 win and $2 place bets (same horse) on the same 15 required races. The contestants who compile the highest total based on mutuel payoffs are the winners. Odds are capped at 20-1 ($42) to win and 10-1 ($22) to place.

Why attend? For only a $50 entry fee, you can shoot for good cash prizes and have a solid chance to qualify for the DRF/NTRA National Handicapping Championship. Each of Prairie Meadows' two contests is limited to 100 participants, but as few as 75 have been known to attend, which gives those who do play an increased chance. The contest pays down to 10 places, and pays back 100 percent of all entry fees to the winners in the form of prize money.

Why not? If you're not from Iowa, Prairie Meadows might not be the most convenient place to get to. If you do go, make sure you have at least a little knowledge of Prairie Meadows' racing, since about two-thirds of the races in the contest will be local events. Also keep in mind that Prairie's second contest (September) is held during their mixed Quarter Horse/Thoroughbred meet, so some background in Quarter Horse handicapping is mandatory if you expect to have a chance.

How to win: Every player in the contest must wager on the same 15 races, meaning that you'll need to connect on a high percentage of winners and hit one or more of the highest-priced winning horses in order to win. However, unlike many contests in which the entire field must play the same races, you might be able to miss one big-odds winner and still be able to win. This is due to the fact that only 75 to 100 people will be in the field. Before you come, familiarize yourself with the racing at Prairie Meadows and shoot for a final total over $130. The winner of Prairie's spring 2002 tournament finished with $151, with $138 (runner-up) needed to qualify. If you're coming to the fall contest, make sure you know a little something about Quarter Horse racing.

Where to stay: Prairie Meadows offers special rates at a pair of hotels practically right next to the racetrack, including the **Settle Inn** (515-967-7888) and the **Heartland Inn** (515-967-2400).

Where to eat: The **Fireside Grille** has a variety of good eats right across the street from the track (523 8th St. SE; 515-967-8122). There's also an **Okoboji Bar and Grill** nearby (multiple locations, call 515-264-9422).

Contact info: Call the track at 515-967-1268 and ask for Carrie LaRue for details on their next contest.

RENO HILTON WINTER CHALLENGE AND THE BRAWL IN THE FALL
*Recommended

Where: Reno Hilton, Reno, Nevada
When: February and September
Who: Each contest limited to 64 entries
How much: $1,500 entry fee
Purse: $96,000
Scoreboard? Final round only
DRF/NTRA qualifying spots: 8 (four in each contest)

Contest Rating:	3
Value Rating:	4
Qualifier Rating:	5 (Ratio – 16:1)

■

The Reno Hilton takes traditional tournament formats and throws them out the window in favor of these two contests, which both feature 64-player tournament-bracket formats. The stock in both the Winter Challenge and the Brawl in the Fall instantly went up when the events were made National Handicapping Championship qualifiers. The 2002 Brawl in the Fall attracted an all-star field including 2001 Handicapper of the Year Judy Wagner and dozens of other handicapping-contest winners and past qualifiers to the National Handicapping Championship.

The format of this contest is quite complex. The 64-player field is drawn into 16 four-person minibrackets. Each player competes against the others in his or her bracket on the first day of the contest, with 16 winners advancing in the "winners' bracket" and the remaining 48 players falling into the "losers' bracket." Players in the losers' bracket can no longer win the contest, but can still finish as high as second place and qualify for the National Handicapping Championship. On Day Two, the 16 winners compete in four groups of four, while the 48 players in the losers' bracket compete in 12 groups of four players each. The winners of the four winners'-bracket contests advance to the final four, and the eventual winner of that bracket earns the $50,000 first prize. The 12 losers from the winners' bracket and the 12 winners from the losers' bracket also all advance to the third day of the contest, where they will compete for places 2 through 10 along with the three losing members of the final four.

The top four finishers from each contest qualify for the National Handicapping Championship and earn additional prize money including $20,000 for second, $10,000 for third, $5,000 for fourth, and $1,850 each for fifth through 10th place.

Here's how the betting works. All entrants must pick one track per day to play, and then must make eight $2 across-the-board bets a day on eight different races from that track. Track circuits open for betting include Maryland, Florida, Louisiana, Chicago, Kentucky, New York, and Northern and Southern California. The highest-scoring player from each foursome is the winner, and will advance to face another three rivals the following day. On the final day of the contest, referred to as the money day, players must play eight races from a selection of 16 chosen by the Reno Hilton's race and sports book staff. All bets must be across the board, and all odds will be capped at 20-1 to win, 15-1 to place, and 10-1 to show.

Why attend? The Reno Hilton's major selling point for these contests is simple, yet effective and truthful: Beat nine people to win $50,000. You're never playing against the entire field of 64 players in these contests. Instead, you are playing against only three other players at any given time. If you beat three groups of three handicappers (3+3+3=9), you win. It's as simple as that. The contest also has a very good prize structure beyond just the grand-prize winner. The top 10 finishers in a field of 64 (15 percent) make at least a small profit.

Why not? You either like this format or you don't. This contest format makes something really difficult out of something really simple. Players compete in brackets and not against the whole field, meaning that people with lower scores can advance to the next round over higher scores. Maybe you don't understand the very complex format of this contest, and don't want to take time to learn. Maybe you can't make it to Reno. Maybe you don't have enough money to cover the $1,500 entry fee.

How to win: It's tough to pin down an exact strategy to try to win this event, because anything can happen in any individual four-person bracket. Past brackets have been won with as little as $17 in earnings or as much as $134. A general rule, however, is to shoot for a total of around $80 (based on $2 across-the-board bets on eight races) in order to win your bracket and advance.

Where to stay: The **Reno Hilton** takes the guesswork out of where to stay. All contest entries include a complimentary room for the duration of the tournament.

Where to eat: All contestants are served breakfast and lunch all three days of the contest, and the Reno Hilton also provides a welcome banquet the night before the contest begins. The Reno Hilton is a large resort property with many fine eateries, so you shouldn't have trouble finding somewhere to have dinner during your stay. Try **The Steak House,** which is known for its blackened prime rib, and **Andiamo**, which serves Mediterranean seafood and pasta in an upscale atmosphere. Call the hotel at 800-501-2651 to make reservations.

Contact info: Call the Reno Hilton's tournament guru, Steve Fierro, at 775-789-2568.

RENO HILTON SUMMER SHOWDOWN

Where: Reno Hilton, Reno, Nevada
When: June
Who: 200 entries
How much: $200 entry fee, $600 real-money buy-in
Purse: $40,000
Scoreboard? No
DRF/NTRA qualifying spots: 4

Contest Rating: 3
Value Rating: 4
Qualifier Rating: 3 (Ratio – 50:1)

■

The premise of this contest is real life, and the format is designed to resemble an actual day at the track as closely as possible. Players enter the contest for a $200 fee, and that money goes into the prize-money pool, which will be $40,000 based on 200 players (all entry fees are returned to the top 10 in the form of prize money). All players then buy in with a $600 real-money bankroll, with the only stipulation being that players must bet exactly $300 on each day of the two-day contest.

Winnings cannot be re-wagered. The daily $300 bankroll can be bet any way you see fit on any bet from any track handled by the Reno Hilton race book (only pick sixes and place pick nines are not allowed). The players who accumulate the highest two-day bankrolls will be the winners, and the top four finishers will all qualify for the National Handicapping Championship. Since all bets are made in real money, all players get to keep their winnings, or take home what's left of their $600 bankroll, at the end of the contest.

Why attend? The Reno Hilton's contests are run by Steve Fierro, a true dyed-in-the-wool handicapper and horseplayer who knows what players want and gives it to them in the form of quality handicapping tournaments. If you bet in the neighborhood of $300 a day on the races, this contest will be just like a normal day at the track.

Why not? Some players prefer a little more structure to the contests they enter. Anything goes in this event, making it difficult to play a winning strategy. Should you plug away with straight wagers, play exactas and trifectas, or shoot for the stars with bets like superfectas and pick fours? This contest doesn't post scores, so you're going to be flying blind not knowing if you need a $10,000 trifecta in order to win.

How to win: Generally speaking, these "anything-goes" real-money contests are played close to the vest. Nobody wants to lose $600 in actual bets by going for 50-1 shots or playing crazy superfecta combinations. It doesn't seem like you would be able to win this kind of contest with straight bets, but that route is often the way to go in real-money tournaments. Pick your best bet of the day in the 10-1 to 20-1 odds range and bet it all on a single horse on each day of the contest. A $300 win bet on a 10-1 horse returns $3,300, and one or two hits on that kind of a horse alone should be enough to land you in the top four and qualify you for the National Handicapping Championship.

Where to stay: The **Reno Hilton** offers reduced rates for tournament players. Call 800-501-2651 for reservations.

Where to eat: There are eight restaurants at the Reno Hilton. Fans of Chinese and Japanese food should try **Asiana**. If you prefer a buffet, the Reno Hilton's **Grand Canyon Buffet** is one of the best in town.

Contact info: Call the Reno Hilton's tournament coordinator, Steve Fierro, at 775-789-2568.

RETAMA PARK'S DRF/NTRA QUALIFIER TOURNAMENTS
*Recommended

Where: Retama Park, Selma, Texas (San Antonio area)
When: August and September
Who: Limited to 200 entries but 100 are more likely (maximum of two entries per person)
How much: $100 entry fee plus a $60 live bankroll
Purse: $11,000 in each contest based on 100 entries
Scoreboard? No
DRF/NTRA qualifying spots: 2 in each contest

Contest Rating:	4
Value Rating:	5
Qualifier Rating:	3 (Ratio – 50:1)

■

Retama Park held this contest for the first time in 2002, but it took no time for the track to get it right. This one-day event is nearly the perfect little contest and is highly recommended for those seeking to qualify for the National Handicapping Championship.

The Retama tournament is actually two separate contests, held about a month apart during Retama's live race meet. Players can enter both contests, and each event has two DRF/NTRA qualifying spots available to the winners. Both contests return all entry fees to the winners in the form of prize money, and Retama also will throw in an additional $1,000 of its own money to the winner. The contests each pay down to fourth place, with 50 percent of the pot plus $1,000 going to the first-place finisher, 30 percent to second, 15 percent to third, and five percent to fourth.

The format of the contest is simple, with players making 15 real-money $2-to-win and $2-to-place bets on the full cards from three tracks. August's contest includes the Retama live card plus simulcasts from Del Mar and Mountaineer Park. September's contest features simulcast wagering on Belmont, Louisiana Downs, and Turfway. The players who accumulate the most earnings based on their $2-to-win, $2-to-place bets will win the tournament, and since contestants are playing for real money, all final balances will be returned to players at the end of the proceedings. Notably, there is no scoreboard used in this contest. Only final scores will be posted at the end of the competition.

Why attend? This contest has a good format and offers tremendous value, with Retama not only returning all entry fees in the form of prize money but also putting an extra $1,000 of its own money into the pot. Since this is a real-money contest, you get to keep whatever you make whether you happen to win or lose.

Why not? The main shortcoming of this format is the fact that the prize structure is a bit top heavy, with only the first four finishers earning prize money. Players who aren't familiar with tracks like Retama, Mountaineer, and Louisiana Downs may be at a disadvantage. Tournament players who prefer contests with score updates may also want to stay away.

How to win: Retama's contest has installed a couple of the best safeguards to insure against blind stabbing on longshots. First, your bankroll is real money, and second, there's no scoreboard. Tournaments like this one tend not to be centered around longshot plays as much as some other types of contests. Concentrate on picking winners, even if that means selecting a few favorites. You'll need some long prices to win, but a few shorties in the mix couldn't hurt. You have 15 real-money $2 win-and-place bets during the contest for a total starting bankroll of $60. Based on past results, you'll probably need to turn that $60 into at least $160 in order to win and/or qualify for Las Vegas.

Where to stay: There are many hotels located close to Retama, including the **La Quinta Inn** (210-657-5500), the **Days Inn Windcrest** (210-650-0779), and the **Drury Inn** (201-654-1144).

Where to eat: After the races, many Retama racetrackers like to head out to the **Louis Ledeaux Cajun Seafood Kitchen** (210-845-8222) in the Forum Shopping Center in nearby Universal City. The **Outback Steakhouse** (8131 Agora Pkwy.; 210-945-8100) is also popular due to its proximity to the track.

Contact info: Call Retama's friendly marketing and publicity department at 210-651-7053 for more information.

RIVER DOWNS/DRF HANDICAPPING CONTEST

Where: River Downs, Cincinnati, Ohio
When: Most-recent contests were May 18, 2002, and August 10, 2002
Who: Field limited to 100. Contests sell out.
How much: Entry fee is $100
Purse: River Downs guarantees $6,800 in prizes in each contest.
Scoreboard? Yes
DRF/NTRA qualifying spots: 2

Contest Rating: 4
Value Rating: 2
Qualifier Rating: 3 (Ratio – 50:1)

■

The River Downs contest is a one-day event held on the third floor of the grandstand on the track's east end. The majority of the entrants in this contest are local Cincinnati and Kentucky horseplayers, with a small number of players also coming in from other parts of the country. Players receive reserved seats, lunch, and free track programs and *Daily Racing Forms*. The purse is $6,800 in cash and players have the chance to win two qualifying spots in the DRF/NTRA National Handicapping Championship.

Players must wager $2 to win and $2 to place on one horse in every designated contest race. Contest races usually consist of the live card and possibly a stakes-race simulcast. The winner is the player who accumulates the most money based on the total payoffs of his selections. Aside from two qualifying slots to the DRF/NTRA National Handicapping Championship, the top four finishers all win cash prizes. The prize breakdown is $5,000 for first, $1,000 for second, $500 for third, and $300 for fourth.

Why attend? Players who have a strong knowledge of racing at River Downs will have an advantage in this contest because the majority of the tournament races are from the live card. The $100 entry fee is affordable for most players, and the prize money is good for the top four finishers. The field is limited to 100 entries (one qualifying spot per 50 entrants), and the field is not filled with elite tournament players.

Why not? This contest doesn't offer good value because River Downs won't be returning 100 percent of the entry fees in the form of prize money unless 68 people or fewer enter. It's tough to make money betting against a 32 percent takeout. (Note: River Downs does reserve the right to increase the amount of prize money.) If you're not familiar with the racing at River Downs, you'll be at a disadvantage against the guys with local knowledge.

How to win: The May 2002 River Downs contest winner, Craig Koff of Highland Beach, Florida, hit eight winners in the 10-race contest including a few good prices. The average winner of this event won't need to hit 80 percent of his selections, but picking winners is the name of the game at this contest. Since everyone in the field must play the same limited amount of races, it's difficult to comb through races and only bet longshots. The format of this sort of contest values picking winners more than similar contests that offer simulcasts from several tracks. Be careful, however, because it is very difficult to win a contest like this if you don't hit the longest-priced winner on card. With 100 players in the field, at least 10 are sure to have even the longest longshot on the card.

Where to stay: The **Radisson Hotel Cincinnati** (859-491-1200) offers a special River Downs rate at a reduced price. **A. J.'s Road House** (513-231-2447) is right next door to River Downs.

Where to eat: Nearby River Downs, **Michael G's** (4601 Kellogg Ave.; 513-533-3131) is the place to go for pasta, seafood, and steaks in a casual atmosphere. Outdoor river-view seating and live music are also available. **Montgomery Inn at the Boathouse** (925 Eastern Ave.; 513-721-7427) is well worth the 15-minute drive from River Downs for world-famous ribs right on the Ohio River.

Contact info: Call the River Downs marketing department at 513-232-8000.

Sam Houston's DRF/NTRA Qualifier Handicapping Tournament

Where: Sam Houston Race Park, Houston, Texas
When: October
Who: Limited to 200 entries
How much: $100 entry fee (early-bird entrants receive a $25 rebate)
Purse: $5,200 guaranteed
Scoreboard? Yes
DRF/NTRA qualifying spots: 4

Contest Rating: 3
Value Rating: 1
Qualifier Rating: 3 (Ratio – 50:1)

■

Sam Houston Race Park hosts a one-day contest to determine all four of its qualifying spots to the National Handicapping Championship. The contest is limited to 200 entries and costs $100 to enter; however, players who enter before the day of the contest receive a $25 rebate in the form of a mutuel betting voucher. The total purse of the tournament is $5,200, with $3,000 going to the winner, $1,000 for second, $500 for third, and $500 for fourth. Additional $100 prizes go to the player who earns the highest total in the contest's mandatory races, and the player who earns the most in the contest's optional plays. All entrants get a free contest program, a seat on the club level, and buffet meal, and a Sam Houston gift bag.

Results of the contest are based on 20 mythical $2 win and $2 place wagers on the races from approximately seven simulcast tracks. Ten of the races are mandatory plays selected by the racetrack, and the other 10 are players'-choice plays on any race at any track offered in the contest. You can expect the mandatory races to be spread out among Arlington, Belmont, Delaware, and Keeneland, while the optional races can be chosen from Louisiana Downs, Remington Park, and Santa Anita. There are odds caps of 25-1 to win and 15-1 to place. Scores are updated after each mandatory race.

Why attend? The Sam Houston tournament features a good, action-filled format with 20 contest races packed into one marathon day of handicapping. Four qualifying spots are offered in a single one-day event, which makes this a good option for out-of-town players as well as local racegoers.

Why not? This tournament's takeout is extremely high based on a full field of 200 entries. If the contest sells out, the takeout will be 65 percent even if the entire field only pays the advance entry price of $75 (200 x $75 = $15,000, but the prize money is only $5,200). Sam Houston offers four DRF/NTRA qualifying spots and some other perks, but from a prize-money perspective, there's no value here. In addition, the prize structure is also top heavy, with only the first four finishers out of a field of 200 earning prizes.

How to win: It will definitely help your chances to bet on, and hit, a few mid- to high-priced winners in this contest because of the big odds caps of 25-1 to win and 15-1 to place. In the past, this contest has been won with a total of $118 (Steven "Rocket" Rosen in October 2000), so plan on needing to triple your bankroll in order to win.

Where to stay: The **Hilton Garden Inn** (832-912-1000) offers a special Sam Houston Race Park rate of $69 per night and also has free shuttle service to the racetrack. Another option somewhat close to the track is the **Holiday Inn-Houston Northwest** (713-939-9955).

Where to eat: One of the best places you can go in the Sam Houston Race Park area is **bw-3's Buffalo Wild Wings** (17195 Tomball Parkway; 281-955-7800) for some of the top-rated chicken wings and burgers in town. A little farther away from the track is **Champps Americana** (1121 Uptown Park Blvd.; 713-627-2333), a sports bar and social gathering place also known for karaoke. If all else fails, there's always **Hooters** (120 FM 1960 Road W.; 281-893-9464).

Contact info: For more information call 281-807-8833.

SANTA ANITA (OAK TREE) HANDICAPPING CONTEST

Where: Santa Anita Park, Arcadia, California
When: October
Who: Anyone can enter. Between 9,000 and 10,000 entries are the norm.
How much: Free
Purse: $10,000
Scoreboard? No
DRF/NTRA qualifying spots: 4

Contest Rating: 2
Value Rating: Free
Qualifier Rating: 1 (Ratio – 2,500:1)

■

Santa Anita hosts an annual free handicapping contest during its fall Oak Tree meet, which attracts between 9,000 and 10,000 entries per year, every year. From that large group, only four players will advance to the DRF/NTRA National Handicapping Championship in Las Vegas. Despite the fact that this contest costs nothing to enter, Santa Anita puts up a pot of $10,000 in prize money for the top 20 finishers with $2,500 going to the winner, $2,000 for second, $1,500 for third, $1,000 for fourth, $750 for fifth, $250 for 6th through 10th, and $100 for 11th through 20th place.

The contest begins with a simple preliminary round where players pick up an entry ballot and select one horse per race in Santa Anita's pick-six races (normally races 4 through 9). If any of an entrant's picks finishes in the money in any of the six races, that player will be invited to participate in the track's final round later in the meet. This means that basically everyone who enters will have the opportunity to return to the track to play in the final round, and roughly half of the 9,000 to 10,000 original players will do so. In the final round, players will again pick a horse in six Santa Anita races. The four entrants whose selections total the most money based on mythical $2 win and $2 place bets will be declared the winners. The track gets to pick which six races are used in the contest, and there is no odds cap on winning payoffs.

Why attend? If you're a regular racegoer at Santa Anita, there is no reason not to submit an entry blank and give it a shot. The contest is free, but still offers prize money of $10,000.

Why not? The odds of winning this contest are so remote that it probably isn't worth it for out-of-towners to make two separate trips to Santa Anita in order to participate.

How to win: Show up for the preliminary round to make yourself eligible. Then shoot for the moon in the final round. There is no odds cap, and you must finish in the top four to qualify or the top 20 to earn prize money. In order to do so in a field this large, you'll need to hit all the highest-priced winners in the contest. If a bunch of favorites win, you'll have to go a perfect 6 for 6.

Where to stay: The **Holiday Inn-Monrovia** (626-357-1900) is the official hotel of Santa Anita and is located just one mile from the racetrack. Ask for the Santa Anita Park horsemen's rate when you call for reservations.

Where to eat: The **Derby** restaurant (233 E. Huntington Dr.; 626-447-8174) in Arcadia has long been identified as the after-the-races destination near Santa Anita. The steakhouse features racetrack memorabilia including photos, saddles, silks, and other racing relics dating back to the 1800's. Another area favorite with the racetrack crowd is the **Outback Steakhouse** (626-447-6435) in Arcadia.

Contact info: Call Santa Anita's marketing department at 626-574-6384 and ask for more information about their next DRF/NTRA handicapping contest.

SPORTS HAVEN'S AUTOTOTE HANDICAPPING CHALLENGE
*Recommended

Where: Sports Haven teletheater, New Haven, Connecticut
When: Early February (the weekend after the Super Bowl)
Who: Maximum 340 entries
How much: $300 entry fee
Purse: $102,000 purse including $40,000 to the winner and payoffs down to 25th place.
Scoreboard? Yes, updated after every bet.
DRF/NTRA qualifying spots: 2

Contest Rating:	5
Value Rating:	4
Qualifier Rating:	2 (Ratio – 170:1)

■

The Sports Haven Handicapping Challenge has become the East's most prestigious handicapping contest since the demise of the World Series of Handicapping at Penn National in 2000. From its inception in 1997, the Sports Haven tournament has sold out every annual contest with players coming from more than 20 different states and Canada.

The Handicapping Challenge is a two-day event involving the full race cards from three tracks—Aqueduct, Gulfstream, and Santa Anita. Players make 10 mythical $200 wagers on each day of the contest. Betting is win, place, and/or show, and must be in $50 increments (example: $100 to win, $50 to place, $50 to show).

One entry is allowed per person unless the contest fails to sell out. All winning payoffs have been capped at 20-1 to win, 10-1 to place, and 5-1 to show ever since Frisk Me Now tilted the tote board at $213 in Gulfstream Park's Hutcheson Stakes on the weekend of the inaugural contest.

The top four finishers qualify for the National Handicapping

Championship, and annually are the first qualifiers for the following year's event.

Why attend? This contest provides a chance to measure your tournament skills against many of the best players in the game. It is perhaps the best and most professionally run contest held anywhere on an annual basis. The $40,000 grand prize is well worth shooting for, and the other cash prizes, which go to everyone in the top 10, aren't bad, either; prize money for second is $15,000, and the awards continue on down to $2,300 for 10th. Also, four qualifying spots in the National Handicapping Championship are on the line.

Autotote takes very good care of its guests, supplying free meals for both days of the contest in addition to complimentary *Daily Racing Forms*. Sports Haven also throws in a gift, such as logo caps or gold shirts, to all 340 entrants. Fans of scoreboards will love the up-to-the-minute, bet-by-bet scorekeeping done by hand on large, easy-to-read boards displayed prominently in the front of the contest area.

Why not? If your goal is strictly to reach the finals of the National Handicapping Championship, this will not be the easiest place to qualify. With 340 entries in the contest, the numerical odds against you finishing among the top four are 170-1. Additionally, many of the best and most successful tournament players from all over the country will be competing against you for the same four spots.

How to win: Since the odds were capped at 20-1 to win, 10-1 to place, and 5-1 to show after the inaugural event, the winners of this contest have totaled $10,965 (Bob Weidlich, 1998), $11,390 (Rick Lang, 1999), $15,260 (Ron Butkiewicz, 2000), $11,430 (Charles Carito, 2001), and $10,320 (Stuart "Beef" Rubin, 2002) for an average of $11,873. In order to build a total that high, a winning player is going to need to bet his whole $200 on each race to win and aim at some longshots hovering around the 20-1 odds cap. Don't bet horses lower than 4-1 or 5-1, and be sure to take advantage of the scoreboard late in the contest and adjust your strategy accordingly.

Keep in mind that the top four finishers qualify for the National Handicapping Championship. The average fourth-place finisher in this contest has bankrolled $9,301, so you'll probably have to beat that number to be on your way to Las Vegas.

Where to stay: The **Marriott Fairfield Inn** (203-562-1111) is just around the corner from Sports Haven, and offers a $69 per night room rate for tournament guests. For those who want to stay in downtown New Haven within walking distance of Yale University, the **New Haven Hotel** (203-498-3288) offers single rooms for $85 during the contest (with parking not included).

Where to eat: For good seafood just across the street from Sports Haven, try the **Rusty Scupper** (501 Long Wharf Dr.; 203-777-5711). You can't go wrong on Wooster Street, New Haven's famous strip of Italian restaurants, which includes **Frank Pepe's Pizzeria** (157 Wooster St., 203-865-5762).

Contact info: Call 203-946-3189 or 203-946-3139, or visit *www. ctotb.com* for more information on this and Autotote's other contests throughout the year.

SUFFOLK DOWNS/NTRA QUALIFYING ROUND

Where: Suffolk Downs, East Boston, Massachusetts
When: November
Who: As many as 400 entries
How much: Two contests with entry fees of either $2 or $25
Purse: $2,500
Scoreboard? Yes
DRF/NTRA qualifying spots: 4 (two contests with two qualifiers each)

Contest Rating:	3
Value Rating:	5
Qualifier Rating:	2 (Ratio – 125:1)

■

For the past several years, Suffolk Downs has hosted two DRF/NTRA qualifying handicapping tournaments per year for a minuscule $2 entry fee. In 2002, Suffolk changed gears a bit by hosting one $2 contest and turning its other event into a more traditional handicapping contest with a larger, but still moderate, entry fee of $25. Both contests offer two qualifying spots to the National Handicapping Championship.

In the $2 contest, players are given an imaginary $1,500 bankroll that is divided into five different win bets in the amounts of $500, $400, $300, $200, and $100. Players may place these wagers in any race on the Suffolk Downs live race card. A contestant may wager on more than one horse in a single race, but may not wager on a single horse more than once by adding together two win-bet denominations. Players are allowed only one entry, and players turning in multiple entries will be disqualified.

This contest normally draws between 300 and 400 entries. The players who accumulate the highest earnings with their allotment of $1,500 in bets will be the winners. There is no prize money available, but the two qualifying trips to the National Handicapping Championship in Las Vegas are more than adequate prizes considering the $2 entry fee.

Suffolk Downs' newer $25 contest involves the same $500 down to $100 wagering format, but in this contest, betting will be on 10 different races including five races from Suffolk Downs and another five (and another set of five bets from $500 to $100) on simulcast races from Aqueduct, Calder, or Churchill. Total prize money for the one-day contest will be $2,500 based on 100 entries. The actual prize money will depend on the final number of entries, with Suffolk paying back 100 percent of all entry fees in the form of prize money.

Why attend? These contests won't cost you a lot of money, but nonetheless will offer a total of four qualifying spots in the National Handicapping Championship. The $2 contest is like a free event for all intents and purposes, but unlike the free racetrack contests in California, you won't need to beat 5,000 to 10,000 people in order to qualify. The unique format of the $2 contest is very interesting and inventive.

Why not? Those who like handicapping-contest competition and atmosphere should stick with Suffolk's more traditional-style $25 entry fee contest. In the $2 entry fee contest, you simply fill out an entry blank and turn it in.

How to win: More historical data is available on the $2 contest, which has been held since 1999. Colin Riley of Weymouth, Massachussets, turned his original $1,500 bankroll into a contest-winning total of $13,060 in November 2000. Second place in that same contest was $10,490. Based on these kinds of totals, you're going to need to multiply your original bankroll by seven in order to qualify. Needless to say, you've got to hit longshots to win, especially with your higher-denomination wagers.

Where to stay: The best place to stay when visiting Suffolk Downs is the **Hampton Inn-Logan Airport** (781-286-5665), which is right across the street from the track. There's also the nearby **Comfort Inn and Suites-Logan Airport** (781-485-3600).

Where to eat: Many people go to **Sablone's** (107 Porter St.; 617-567-8140) for Italian food close to the track. For the best barbecue in town, try **UNCLE Pete's Hickory Ribs** (309 Bennington St.; 617-

569-7427). Up the road in Saugus, Massachusetts, is the **Hilltop Steakhouse** (855 Broadway; 781-233-7000). Courageous fans of dive bars might want to check out the **Esquire Club** (297 Lee Burbank Hwy.; 781-284-9650) across the street from the track.

Contact info: Call Suffolk Downs at 617-568-3323 for more details.

SUNLAND PARK DRF/NTRA QUALIFYING TOURNAMENT
*Recommended

Where: Sunland Park (El Paso, Texas area)
When: July or August
Who: About 100 players, but recent contests have had as few as 52 entrants
How much: Entry fee is $20 (two entries per person are allowed)
Purse: $2,000 based on a field of 100
Scoreboard? Verbal updates after mandatory races
DRF/NTRA qualifying spots: 4

Contest Rating:	4
Value Rating:	5
Qualifier Rating:	5 (Ratio – 25:1)

■

The Sunland Park DRF/NTRA Qualifying Tournament is one of the best-kept secrets on the road to the National Handicapping Championship. This little gem of a contest costs only $20 to enter ($40 for late entries) and gives players a good, inexpensive chance to qualify for a trip to the national finals. Expect a field of about 100 players based on 2002's figures (99 entries), but as recently as 2000, only 52 players vied for four available DRF/NTRA qualifying spots. Clearly, the secret is getting out that this contest is a great place to go to qualify. Besides offering favorable qualifying odds, Sunland Park also puts on a fun tournament and pays back 100 percent of all entry fees in the form of prize money. As an added perk, Sunland throws in a free Quarter Horse contest entry to every participant. The winner of that event advances to the final of the AQHA's DRF/NTRA qualifying handicapping contest.

The format of the two-day contest is a familiar one, but a good one nonetheless. Players must make 15 mythical $2-to-win and $2-to-place bets per day on the races from Arlington, Del Mar, Louisiana Downs, Ruidoso, and Saratoga (Sunland is dark during the contest). The bets are divided into eight mandatory wagers and seven optional wagers per day, and the top four finishers based on winning mutuel prices split the majority of the prize money and earn trips to the National Handicapping Championship in Las Vegas. The prize money is paid down to sixth place with 50 percent going to first, 25 percent to second, 13 percent to third, 7 percent to fourth, 3 percent to fifth, and 2 percent to sixth. Notably, there is no odds cap in this tournament.

Why attend? Attendees get a great (and cheap) shot to qualify for the National Handicapping Championship, and get to play in a contest with a good format and no takeout, to boot. When you're done with the contest, slot machines beckon next door.

Why not? Sunland Park, New Mexico, might be too far out of the way for some tournament players to travel for a shot at the big time. Making a trip to a faraway track that has no live racing at the time is not some people's idea of fun. No odds cap is a definite negative.

How to win: Be sure to buy the maximum two entries; it'll only cost you $40. Standard tournament strategy applies with contest plays recommended on horses at 5-1 or better. Be mindful of longshots and the lack of an odds cap, but don't automatically go overboard with 40-1 horses as a result. You may give yourself a better chance at qualifying with mid-priced horses if only 100 or so contestants show up. The format starts you with $120, and a final tally of $300 or more was needed to qualify in 2002 after the winner hit a 90-1 horse. Plenty of sharpies are likely to be in attendance, so you can count on needing to at least double your bankroll, and maybe even triple it in order to punch your ticket to Las Vegas.

Where to stay: The closest hotels are about a mile away over the Texas border in El Paso. Sunland arranges a special $49 contest rate at the **Holiday Inn Sunland Park** (915-833-2900). The **Best Western Sunland Park Inn** (915-587-4900) is also in the area.

Where to eat: Nearby restaurants include **Dona Chole Tortillas and Tostadas** (1809 McNutt Rd.; 505-874-1198) and **Paquime Trading Company** (1324 McNutt Rd.; 505-589-3484).

Contact info: Call Sunland Park at 505-874-5205 for details.

THISTLEDOWN HANDICAPPING CONTEST

Where: Thistledown, Cleveland, Ohio
When: October and November
Who: Two contests, each limited to 60 entries
How much: $50 entry fee
Purse: $2,300 for each contest
Scoreboard? Yes
DRF/NTRA qualifying spots: 4 (two in each of two contests)

Contest Rating:	3
Value Rating:	3
Qualifier Rating:	4 (Ratio – 30:1)

■

After hosting DRF/NTRA qualifying handicapping contests from 1999 through 2001, Thistledown canceled its contests in 2002. However, the track is expected to revive the contests once again in 2003 and beyond.

In the past, Thistledown was a good place to go to try and qualify for the National Handicapping Championship. The track hosted two annual contests limited to only 60 entries each. The contests cost just $50 to enter, and both offered two qualifying spots to the national finals in addition to prize money. The expense-paid trips to Las Vegas were the only prizes for the top two finishers. The cash purse of $2,300 was divided between the third- through 20th-place finishers.

Contestants in these one-day events try to build the highest bankroll based on $2-to-win and $2-to-place bets on the day's full card of 14 races from Thistledown and Beulah (seven and seven). All payoffs are capped at 20-1, and all win and place wagers must be made on the same horse.

Why attend? This is a good, inexpensive contest that offers players an excellent chance to qualify for the national championship. Good local knowledge of Ohio racing will give you a big leg up on the out-of-town competition. The prize structure is well thought out and not top heavy. Top nonqualifying finishers split all the money, and one-third of the entire field gets a check at the conclusion of the contest.

Why not? If you don't know a little something about Ohio racing, it's going to be very difficult to beat those who do. This contest does not pay out 100 percent of all entry fees in the form of prize money, but that is not a major knock in this case since the dollar amounts involved are so small.

How to win: Players cannot buy two entries for a single contest, but they are allowed to buy one entry each in Thistledown's two contests, which is almost as good. Past editions have been won with totals as high as $101.80, but earnings of at least $81.20 have almost always been enough to finish in the top two and qualify for a trip to Las Vegas.

Where to stay: The closest hotels to Thistledown include the **Courtyard by Marriott-Independence** (216-901-9989), the **Residence Inn by Marriott-Beachwood** (216-831-3030), and the **Embassy Suites-Beachwood** (216-765-8068).

Where to eat: How could a place called **Ms. Que's Rib Factory** (21700 Miles Rd.; 216-581-7427) possibly be bad?

Contact info: Call Thistledown at 216-662-8600 to inquire if they will be hosting any future handicapping contests.

TURF PARADISE REGIONAL DRF/NTRA HANDICAPPING TOURNAMENT
*Recommended

Where: Turf Paradise, Phoenix, Arizona
When: December
Who: Limited to 200 entries (up to two entries per person)
How much: $300 entry fee (late entries cost $400)
Purse: $65,000
Scoreboard? Yes, updates after each race
DRF/NTRA qualifying spots: 8

Contest Rating: 4
Value Rating: 5
Qualifier Rating: 5 (Ratio – 25:1)

■

Turf Paradise racetrack in Phoenix is committed to hosting high-quality handicapping contests, and it shows in their annual Regional DRF/NTRA Qualifying Tournament, which has become one of the top handicapping contests in the country over the past four years. This contest originally became popular because its December spot on the calendar made it one of the last chances of the year to qualify for the National Handicapping Championship. Through the years, Turf Paradise has continually sweetened the pot to the point where this contest is now one of the most looked-forward-to handicapping events of the year.

Besides the fact that this is a well-run contest with a lot of prize money at stake, two bonuses make this contest stand out above all the rest: 1) In 2002, Turf Paradise began offering eight qualifying spots to the National Handicapping Championship, four more than most tracks; 2) Turf Paradise not only pays out 100 percent of all entry fees in the form of prize money, but also adds $5,000 of its own money to the pot, meaning that it pays out 108 percent of everything it takes in. This contest is highly recommended and should not be missed.

The Turf Paradise Handicapping Tournament is limited to 200 entries, with up to two entries allowed per person. The contest costs $300 to enter unless you enter less than one week before the start of the contest, in which case the entry fee becomes $400. The total purse is $65,000 based on a full field, with $26,000 going to the winner, $13,000 for second, $6,500 for third and fourth, and $3,250 each for fifth through eighth place. Two $1,000 daily prizes are also awarded.

Players must make mythical $2-to-win and $2-to-place wagers on one horse in each live Turf Paradise race on both days of the two-day contest. Winners will be determined by adding the combined mutuel payoffs of all a player's selections throughout the two-day event. Payoffs are capped at 20-1 ($42) to win and 10-1 ($22) to place. Scores are updated and posted after every race along with a "Meet Your Fellow Handicappers" list containing the names, hometowns, and occupations of everyone in the contest.

Why attend? Good contest, good value (108 percent payout), eight DRF/NTRA qualifying spots. What more do you need to know?

Why not? The only flaw in this contest's format is the limited amount of races available for betting. Only Turf Paradise races are open for play in the contest, and every player must play every race. Everyone plays the same races, and every race is mandatory.

How to win: First you'd better learn a little something about racing at Turf Paradise, since those are the races you'll be playing. It's all right to play a few well-bet horses in this contest just to bump up your bankroll a few bucks. But beware. With everyone playing the same races, you'll probably need to hit the two or three highest-priced winners during the two-day contest in order to win. This event has been won with a total as high as $298.60 (Bill Wimberley of Phoenix in December 2000) or as low as $164.80 (Bob Hoskins of Port Orchard, Washington, in 1999), so final scores will be hard to predict and depend entirely on the odds of the horses that happen to win during the two-day contest.

Where to stay: The **Comfort Inn Turf Paradise** (602-866-2089) is located adjacent to the racetrack on Bell Road. There's also the convenient **La Quinta Inn Phoenix North** (602-993-0800) located less than a mile away.

Where to eat: Right across the street from Turf Paradise is **Bill Johnson's Big Apple** (16810 N. 19th Ave.; 602-863-7921), a popular place for track-goers looking for barbecued ribs and steaks after the races. There's also **Lenny Monti's Restaurant** (12025 N. 19th Ave.; 602-997-5844). Lenny Monti was the owner of one of the best local racehorses in recent memory, Last Don B.

Contact info: Call Turf Paradise's tournament organizers at 602-375-6464 or 602-375-6462.

TURFWAY HANDICAPPING BLOWOUT

Where: Turfway Park, Florence, Kentucky
When: March, September, and December
Who: Each contest limited to 350 entries
How much: $100 to enter
Purse: $15,000 guaranteed prize money per contest
Scoreboard: Yes, race-by-race updates
DRF/NTRA qualifying spots: 4 total from three contests

Contest Rating:	3
Value Rating:	1
Qualifier Rating:	3 (Ratio – 50:1)

■

Turfway Park hosts three Handicapping Blowouts a year to determine its four qualifiers for the National Handicapping Championship, with the winners from the first two contests and the top two finishers from the December contest all earning trips to the Las Vegas finals. The contests each cost $100 to enter and are limited to 350 entries, with up to three entries allowed per person, per contest. Turfway guarantees prize money of $15,000 regardless of how many actually enter. This prize structure could work strongly to the players' disadvantage, but usually doesn't, with contests generally attracting in the neighborhood of 150 to 180 entries. Turfway's December contest, which offers two DRF/NTRA qualifying spots, usually draws a slightly bigger crowd and is annually one of the last chances for players to earn a trip to the national finals.

The formats of the one-day contests are straightforward, with entrants starting with a mythical $40 bankroll that must be wagered in $2-to-win and $2-to-place increments on 10 live races from Turfway Park. Win and place wagers do not need to be on the same horse. The winner of each contest receives a $10,000 cash grand prize, with $3,000 for second, $1,400 for third, $500 for fourth, and $100 for fifth.

Why attend? The contest costs only $100 per entry, and contestants are allowed to play up to three entries in each contest. If you know one of these contests will only draw its usual 150 to 160 entries (or fewer), then you are assured of a good deal with $15,000 in prize money offered as well as at least one spot in the National Handicapping Championship. Additional prize drawings and money drawings are also offered throughout each contest.

Why not? This contest is very top heavy, with 66 percent of the total prize money plus a DRF/NTRA qualifying spot all going to the winner of each contest. The remainder of the top five finishers split $5,000 in prizes, and the rest of the field leaves empty-handed. If the maximum number of 350 entries were received for a contest, the prize money would still remain at $15,000, meaning the takeout would be astronomical. Also, no matter how many people enter, only the top five earn prize money.

How to win: This format is fairly straightforward, so you would play this contest in much the same way you'd play any $2-to-win, $2-to-place tournament. Past winners have compiled as much as $166.20 (Bill Webber in December 1999) and $162 (Don "Hee Haw" Alvey in September 2000) in earnings, but this event has also been won with as little as $117.40 (Alan Wheeler in October 1999). Aim for a final total of around $160 just to be sure, and/or cross your fingers you can qualify with a smaller amount.

Where to stay: Turfway Park is just down the road from the Cincinnati airport, so there are numerous hotel chains to choose from in the area. A couple good options are the **Marriott Cincinnati Airport** (859-586-0266), which is three miles away from the track in Hebron, Kentucky, and the **Holiday Inn Cincinnati Airport** (859-371-2233) just two miles away from the track in Erlanger, Kentucky.

Where to eat: Many fans of Turfway Park head to the **Tumbleweed**

Southwest Grill (7484 Turfway Road; 859-282-7770) before or after the races for what they call cowboy cuisine including mesquite-grilled steaks and heaping portions of pork and beans. **Eddie's Southern Style Bar-B-Q** (7143 Manderlay Dr.; 859-525-0771) is also worth a visit.

Contact info: Call 859-647-4718 for details.

Twin Spires Club National Handicapping Championship Qualifiers

Where: All Twin Spires Club locations, including Arlington, Calder, Churchill, and Hoosier racetracks, plus off-track locations including Arlington Heights, Chicago, Rockford, Quad Cities, and Waukegan in Illinois; Fort Wayne, Indianapolis, and Merrillville in Indiana; and Louisville, Kentucky.
When: Sundays in September and December
Who: Open to all Twin Spires Club members (membership is free)
How much: Free entry (must be at a Twin Spires Club track or OTB)
Purse: $1,000 in weekly cash prizes at tracks, $250 weekly at OTB's.
Scoreboard? No
DRF/NTRA Qualifying spots: 8

Contact Rating: 2
Value Rating: Free
Qualifier Rating: 2 (Ratio – 100:1)

■

The Twin Spires Club, the player-reward program for Arlington, Calder, Churchill, and Hoosier, gives its members eight separate opportunities throughout the fall to qualify for the National Handicapping Championship and earn additional prize money. All contests cost nothing to enter. Contestants are required to be members of the Twin Spires Club, but membership in the club is also free of charge. The qualifying events are held on four Sundays in September before Churchill's live fall meet, and four Sundays in December following Churchill's fall meet. One DRF/NTRA qualifying spot will be available to the winner of each contest, plus the Twin Spires Club also throws in up to $1,000 in cash prizes and $500 in traveling money to the winner.

The format of each weekly tournament asks entrants to select a horse in four designated races from a Churchill Downs Simulcast Network racetrack. Players are awarded points based on the finish position of their selection. Five points are awarded for a win, three points are awarded for place, and one point is awarded for show. The player with the most points from all the participating locations combined is that week's grand-prize winner.

Why attend? This is a free contest that is convenient for players in several different areas, including Chicago, Miami, Louisville, and central Indiana. You can join every week for a total of eight chances to qualify for the National Handicapping Championship. Admission to the contest is limited to Twin Spires Club members, and is a good free perk of the club. If you live in one of those areas and attend the track or one of its OTB's, it's worth joining the club to earn reward perks including admission to these contests.

Why not? You need to be on-site in order to participate. Since this contest is open to all Twin Spires Club members at 12 different sites simultaneously, it may not be worth making a special trip for what amounts to a small chance at winning the grand prize. A small entry fee in this case could actually make the contest more attractive to potential entrants by keeping the field size down slightly. This contest also lacks any real tournament atmosphere since entrants are simply handing in entry blanks at different locations all across the country.

How to win: Mutuel prices of winners mean little in this contest, since points are awarded based only on whether your selections run first, second, or third. Since winners paying $4 are worth the same as winners paying $40, there's no reason to play longshots in this contest. Play your best four horses, and hope you can go 4 for 4 because you'll need to in order to have a chance. In case of a tie, the tie-breaker will be a selection on a fifth and final race. You'll probably need to hit that race, too, in order to win over a weekly field in the neighborhood of 800 players.

Contact info: The Twin Spires Club can be reached at 502-638-3881. The website at *www.twinspiresclub.com* is also a good source of information.

WOODBINE THOROUGHBRED HANDICAPPING CHALLENGE

Where: Woodbine, Toronto, Canada
When: August
Who: Limited to 300
How much: $250 entry fee
Purse: $75,000 based on a full field
Scoreboard? Yes
DRF/NTRA qualifying spots: 4

Contest Rating: 4
Value Rating: 4
Qualifier Rating: 3 (Ratio – 75:1)

■

The Woodbine Thoroughbred Handicapping Challenge is Canada's only qualifying contest for the National Handicapping Championship. The contest debuted in 2002 with a big tournament atmosphere and a big purse structure to match. With an entry fee of $250, a maximum of 300 contestants can vie for $75,000 in prize money with $30,000 going to the winner and payoffs down to 10th place. There is a limit of one entry per person, but players may opt to purchase another entry if the contest does not sell out. There is no takeout, with 100 percent of all entry fees being returned to the winners in the form of prize money.

The Woodbine Thoroughbred Handicapping Challenge is a two-day contest. Players make 10 mythical $2 win bets (no place) per day on their choice of races from Woodbine, Fort Erie, and Saratoga. The winner is determined by the highest combined earnings from all wagers based on Woodbine's parimutuel pools for all tracks involved. All payoffs are capped at 20-1 odds ($42). In addition to prize money, the top four finishers will all advance to the DRF/NTRA National Handicapping Championship in Las Vegas. This contest accepts all players 18 and older, but players must still be 21 or older to advance to the National Handicapping Championship.

Why attend? This is a big contest with a good purse that returns 100 percent of all entry fees in the form of prize money. It features betting on both Woodbine and Fort Erie. Therefore, if you live in Canada and/or follow Canadian racing, this could be your best chance to qualify for the National Handicapping Championship. If you don't follow Canadian racing, you still have the option of betting the simulcasts from Saratoga.

Why not? If you know nothing about Canadian racing and don't feel like dipping your toes into the water even just a little, you're going to be extremely limited in the races you can play and may be at a disadvantage to those with a good amount of local knowledge. With 300 players going for four DRF/NTRA qualifying spots, the odds against you qualifying will be 75-1.

How to win: There will be a big field in this event, so you know you'll need a healthy final total if you hope to advance to the National Handicapping Championship. The format is $2 win bets with no place wagers, but you can't let that fact keep you from betting longshots and price horses at 5-1 odds or higher. In order to win, you'll probably need to reach a total of at least $100 based on $2 win bets on 20 races during the two-day contest. Your bankroll probably won't reach $100 without at least a couple winning longshots.

Where to stay: The nearby **Holiday Inn Toronto Airport East** (416-240-7511) offers a special contest rate of $105 a night. Call and ask for the Woodbine Racetrack discount rate. If you prefer to stay farther away from the airport, the **Travelodge Airport Hotel** (416-740-9500) is very close to the track, and even less expensive. The Travelodge is also home to the **Swiss Pick Restaurant**.

Where to eat: After the races, many Woodbine race-goers head to **JJ Muggs Grille and Bar** at the Woodbine Centre Mall (500 Rexdale Blvd.; 416-674-5450). Another good option is **Le Biftheque Steakhouse** (25 Carlson Court; 416-798-4333), a restaurant with a racetrack theme.

Contact info: If you have any questions, call 416-675-3993, ext. 2513 or 2210.

OTHER HANDICAPPING CONTESTS AND TOURNAMENTS

Las Vegas Contests

THE CHAMPIONSHIP AT THE ORLEANS

Where: The Orleans, Las Vegas
When: April and October
Who: Usually 400 to 500 entries
How much: $500 entry fee
Purse: $200,000 based on 400 entries
Information: Call 888-566-7223

The Championship at the Orleans is the biggest and most prestigious non-invitational handicapping contest in the country. The twice-annual event regularly draws over 400 players and pays out six-figure first prizes. Contestants make 12 mythical $100 win wagers per day at six designated tracks on each day of the three-day competition. This contest features a "soft odds cap" with full track odds paid on the first $20, and the remainder paid at a limit of 20-1. Point totals accumulate over the three-day contest, and the players with the highest final bankrolls will be the winners. Payoffs are made as far down as 100th place. The tournament also features $10,000 per day in prize money and a separate $20,000 early-bird contest. All daily and early-bird prize money is furnished by the Orleans. This contest is not a DRF/NTRA National Handicapping Championship qualifying event.

PICK THE PONIES INVITATIONAL

Where: Las Vegas Hilton
When: Kentucky Derby and Breeders' Cup weekends
Who: Limited to 200 entries (maximum of three entries per person)
How much: $500 entry fee ($400 for early-bird entries)
Purse: All entry fees plus $15,000 are returned in the form of prize money
Information: Call 702-735-0101 for details.

■

Based on an entry fee of $500 and a full field of 200 players, the Pick the Ponies Invitational could offer prize money as high as $100,000. Players make 10 mythical $100 across-the-board wagers on 10 different races a day for three days. The winner earns 38 percent of the prize pool, or $38,000, based on a $100,000 purse. Payoffs are made down to 30th place. The Las Vegas Hilton throws in additional daily prize money of $15,000. Through 2002, this contest was not a DRF/NTRA qualifier.

SUPER TOURNAMENT AT THE SUNCOAST

Where: The Suncoast, Las Vegas (Summerlin, Nevada)
When: January and August
Who: 200 entries
How much: $500 entry fee
Purse: $175,000 (based on 200 entries)
Information: Call 888-566-7223

■

The Suncoast Invitational is the younger, smaller, and slightly more expensive sister contest to the Championship at the Orleans. As in its fellow Coast Resorts tournament at the Orleans, Super Tournament players also make 9 mythical $100 win bets on each day of the contest at designated contest tracks. The Suncoast also kicks in an additional $75,000 in added money. Full track odds are paid on the first $20, after which payoffs are capped at 20-1.

Online Contests

AQHA DASH TO THE CHALLENGE ONLINE CONTEST

Where: www.aqha.com/racing
When: May through September
Who: 3,000 estimated entrants
How much: Free
Purse: $1,750
Information: Go to *www.aqha.com/racing*

■

The Dash to the Challenge on-line contest is a nine-race event intended to test one's Quarter Horse handicapping skills. The nine races are all key Quarter Horse stakes races spread out over a three-month period between Memorial Day and Labor Day. Entrants log on to the American Quarter Horse Association's web site to try to select the winner of each contest race. Points are awarded based on actual mutuel payoffs of mythical $2 across-the-board wagers. The winner earns $1,000 and also qualifies for the DRF/NTRA National Handicapping Championship. The second-place finisher earns $500, and the third-place finisher takes home $250.

AQHA Dash to the Challenge On-Track Contest

Where: Remington Park, Retama, Delta Downs, Les Bois Park, Sam Houston, Wyoming Downs, Evergreen Park, Sunland, Canterbury, Ruidoso, Los Alamitos, Blue Ribbon Downs, Fair Meadows, Turf Paradise
When: May through November
Who: 1000 estimated entrants
How much: Free
Purse: $1,000
Information: Go to www.aqha.com/racing for information on this and other AQHA contests

■

Racetracks across the U.S. and Canada will be holding regional on-track Dash to the Challenge contests throughout the year. One winner at each track will receive a free trip, including airfare and hotel, to attend the MBNA Challenge Championships at Lone Star Park at Grand Prairie, Texas, in November. Tracks offer prizes for second- and third-place finishers, and some kick in additional prize money for first place. On the night of the MBNA Challenge at Lone Star Park, AQHA will hold the finals of the Dash to the Challenge contest. Only the winners from the regional contests will be eligible for the final. The winner of that final will earn the title of Champion American Quarter Horse Handicapper plus $1,000 cash, a trophy, and an entry in the DRF/NTRA National Handicapping Championship. The formats of the regional contests will vary, so contact the participating racetracks for more information.

BRISnet.com Online Handicapping Challenge

Where: www.brisnet.com
When: April and October-November
Who: Unlimited
How much: Free, but players must buy past performances
Purse: $25,000
Information: Go to www.brisnet.com

■

Bloodstock Research Information Systems (BRIS) hosts two on-line handicapping contests a year, each offering $25,000 in total prize money. Through 2002, these contests have been qualifying events for the

National Handicapping Championship. In both events, entrants attempt to pick the winners of 10 preselected races every Saturday for the one-month duration of the contest. Players earn one point as well as a point total equal to the $2 win mutuel for each winning selection. The player with the most accumulated points over the course of the contest will be the grand-prize winner of $5,000. The player with the highest accumulated bankroll throughout the contest will be the runner-up and also earn $5,000. Weekly prizes will also be awarded for most winners and highest bankroll.

NATIONAL THOROUGHBRED RACING ASSOCIATION/ BREEDERS' CUP ONLINE CHALLENGE

Where: www.ntra.com
When: September through the Breeders' Cup
Who: Unlimited
How much: Free
Purse: $10,000
Information: Go to www.ntra.com

■

The NTRA and Breeders' Cup Ltd. have held DRF/NTRA qualifying contests each of the last two years. The 2001 contest was the Breeders' Cup Fantasy, an online fantasy-stable game. The 2002 contest featured two phases beginning with the "Head2Head" match-up wager. There were approximately 20 Head2Head races in this phase of the competition. Players were able to earn points based on their Head2Head selections, with one point awarded for each correct selection in the Head2Head match-ups. The top four finishers at the end of this match-up phase earned berths into the 2003 DRF/NTRA National Handicapping Championship in Las Vegas. Phase Two was a "Pick Eight," which began shortly after the post-position draw on the Wednesday before the Breeders' Cup World Thoroughbred Championships. The Pick Eight phase of the contest gave players the chance to make one win selection for the eight Breeders' Cup races with a grand prize of $10,000 guaranteed for the player or players with the highest level of correct selections. Limit of one guess per player. Go to *www.ntra.com* for the rules of this year's NTRA/Breeders' Cup competition.

Phone Betting

AUTOTOTE ON THE WIRE PHONE WAGERING TOURNAMENT

Where: 800-486-2260
When: Four contests annually
Who: Available to residents of 28 states where telephone betting is legal
How much: $200 entry fee, which also serves as betting bankroll
Purse: $5,000 for each of four contests
Information: Call customer service at 800-468-2260 or log on to www.ctotb.com.

■

Autotote's Connecticut OTB telephone-wagering service offers four handicapping contests a year. The winner of each earns first prize of $2,000 and qualifies for the National Handicapping Championship. The contest is open to anyone with an On the Wire phone-wagering account, and new sign-ups are encouraged and welcome to participate. Entry fee for the one-day contests is $200, which also serves as a player's bankroll. Contestants can make any type of wager, including exotics, on any track handled by the phone service. At the end of the day, the person with the most money wins. Prizes are also offered for second through fifth place, with $1,500 going to the runner-up, $750 for third, $500 for fourth, and $250 for fifth.

New Contests

CAPITAL OTB CHALLENGE

Where: Capital OTB, Albany, New York
When: Spring and fall
Who: 150 players
How much: $100 entry fee
Purse: $15,000
Information: Call Capital OTB's marketing department at (518) 344-5272.

■

Capital OTB hosts handicapping contests at its Albany Teletheater twice a year in April and November. Entrants make 10 mythical $200 win or place bets on the races from New York and Kentucky on each day of the two-day contests. If the Challenge is fully subscribed with 150 entries, there will be a purse of $15,000 with 100 percent of all entry fees returned to the top 10 finishers in the form of prize money. First prize is $6,000. Capital OTB gives free *Daily Racing Forms* to all entrants and offers reduced hotel rates at the nearby **Quality Inn** in Albany.

GOLDEN STATE REWARDS NETWORK CALIFORNIA CUP CHALLENGE

Where: www.gsrn.com
When: November
Who: Members of the Golden State Rewards Network program
How much: Free
Purse: Call for details
Information: Go to *www.gsrn.com*

∎

Golden State Rewards Network, California's statewide on-track and off-track player-rewards program, hosted its first contest in late 2002. The contest was open to registered card-holders. The contest offered four qualifying spots in the DRF/NTRA National Handicapping Championship.

MOHEGAN SUN HANDICAPPING CONTEST

Where: Mohegan Sun, Uncasville, Connecticut
When: March
Who: Open to all customers
How much: Free
Purse: $10,000
Information: Call the Mohegan Sun Race Book at 888-226-7711, ext. 7608.

∎

Mohegan Sun, a Native American-owned and -operated casino/resort in southeast Connecticut, is scheduled to host a free one-day handicapping contest in March. The contest is free to enter and will offer prize money of $10,000 to be divided among the top finishers.

Mohegan Sun has held several handicapping contests in recent years including a DRF/NTRA qualifying contest in 2000. In 2002, the Mohegan Sun Race Book hosted the East Coast Classic, which offered a purse of $110,545 and attracted 73 entries. The resort property, which now includes a new 34-story, 1,176-room hotel, plans more contests in the future to keep up with the increasing demand for handicapping tournaments.

ABOUT THE AUTHOR

Harold Roth/Horsephotos

NOEL MICHAELS IS the online editor of *Daily Racing Form*, America's premier publication covering the sport of Thoroughbred horse racing. Michaels has covered handicapping tournaments for DRF since the start of the National Handicapping Championship in 1999.

Noel Michaels is a native of Skokie, Illinois, a suburb of Chicago. He attended college at the University of Arizona, where he earned a bachelor's degree in Animal Science in 1993. Michael's currently lives in Westbury, New York with his wife, fellow *Daily Racing Form* reporter Karen M. Johnson. Michaels's father-in-law, Hall of Fame trainer P. G. Johnson, is the breeder, trainer, and co-owner of 2002 Breeders' Cup Classic winner Volponi.